HEAVEN
HIKES

HEAVEN HIKES

Father's Sunrise After Son's Rise

JARROD KUHN

Heaven Hikes™

Jarrod Kuhn, Jr.

Jillian Kuhn

ISBN: 979-8-218-83677-1
Printed in the United States of America
First Edition: January 2026

All cover and interior illustrations are original works created under the direction of the author.
All artwork © 2026 by Jarrod Kuhn.
Book design by Jarrod Kuhn.
Set in Garamond.
Printed by Vireo Lex Media.

To Erin—
without you I'd be lost in the wilderness.

To the Fab Five—
our love has moved hearts and mountains.

To my Angel—
you're with me every step of the way.

"For I know the plans I have for you," declares the Lord, "plans to prosper you and not to harm you, plans to give you hope and a future."

—*Jeremiah 29:11*

CONTENTS

Foreword

A Daughter's Note by Jillian Kuhn

At the age of twelve, losing my brother was truly life-altering. He was my best friend, even though at times we didn't understand each other, which is pretty normal for siblings. And even though I was his older sister and was supposed to be the one protecting him, most nights I was the one sleeping in his room because I was too scared to sleep alone. Some nights he'd get frustrated with me, but he always let me stay.

We had Nerf gun wars in the hallway, with my long zebra-print body pillow wedged between us as a barrier. We wrestled, too, me on my knees so I could be his height, going through round after round. He made me laugh harder than anyone ever has. He made everyone laugh; true beacon of light.

I lost him at a time when I didn't even know who I was yet. Grieving at such a young age is especially hard because it's such a heavy emotion when you're still trying to understand the "why" behind the normal feelings you're already experiencing. It's also difficult to grieve while watching your parents struggle. When you're a kid, your parents are supposed to be your heroes, invincible, never showing pain. Losing my brother meant watching them endure an unimaginable amount of hurt.

This book dives deeper into my dad's journey through grief, something I witnessed from the outside. Even though we were all hurting, my dad found peace in the mountains. They became his sanctuary, the one place where he could finally breathe again. I didn't understand this at first, but as I grew older, I realized he was searching for moments where he felt lighter, as close as possible to his son.

I experienced parts of that journey with him, even though hiking was never really my cup of tea. I was becoming a teenager, and the last thing I wanted to do was go on a hike. Still, I went sometimes, because I could see how much it meant to him. I remember one trip up the Palm Springs tramway. We rode to the top, took a mellow hike, and just talked. It was simple, but it was beautiful, a quiet blend of both of our worlds.

There were also times we took on much more aggressive hikes, like The Narrows. Walking stick in hand, I trudged through knee-deep water just to see the smile on his face. Those moments stay with me, not because I loved the hike, but because I loved seeing him feel even a small sense of peace.

It wasn't just hiking that helped him. My dad found comfort in being active and spending time outdoors. He developed a passion for biking. He'd put on his cycling outfit, his helmet, and these dorky headphones that wrapped around his neck. Whenever I saw him getting ready for a ride, I'd giggle, not yet understanding the purpose behind it. As I got older, I finally did.

I grieved very differently. I threw myself into friend groups and distractions, and I didn't begin unpacking my grief until much later, when I started going to therapy. That's when I began seeing connections between my dad's journey and my own that I'd never noticed before. From giggling in the hallway as he left for a bike ride, to standing knee-deep in rushing water in The Narrows, we were both grieving in our own ways. I think that's the strange beauty of it.

Heaven Hikes is a story of highs and lows, not just the kind you find on mountaintops. My father is raw and honest about his journey through the grief of losing his son, hoping that by sharing his story, he might help someone else who's hurting. Not too long ago, he told me, "The reason I'm writing this book is to help at least one person. That's all I want." Wherever you are right now, I hope this book does that for you.

Grieving someone, at any age, is a heavy weight to carry. One of the things that makes it a little easier is realizing you're not the only one who feels this way. As you read, I hope you allow yourself to connect with this story and feel close to the experiences within it. Remember, everyone grieves differently, but you are never alone.

I wish you the best on your journey, and I hope my family's experience brings even a small amount of light to yours.

Jillian Kuhn

Preface

On May 18, 2012, my son, Jarrod Kuhn Jr., left my world for another. He was two months shy of his ninth birthday. My love for Jarrod is as far-reaching and ever-growing as the universe is expansive and without end. When the sun rises or sets, whatever shines or glows, I see it as a gift on my ongoing walk toward closeness with Jarrod's heavenly spirit.

Born in Newport Beach, California, on July 15, 2003, God called Jarrod home after only eight years, ten months, and three days. Each day I held him in my arms, every moment together painted the greatest joys of my life. When I was Jarrod's age, I remember being taught that the way to recall the colors of the rainbow was with the name *Roy G. Biv*, for red, orange, yellow, green, blue, indigo, and violet. About forty-five years later, the rainbow Jarrod has shown me holds colors I never could have imagined.

This book is my story, as Jarrod's dad, on an odyssey toward heavenly closeness. It is a work in progress much of the time. It is a blend of joy and pain all of the time.

After fourteen years, what fills these pages is how time has unfolded for me. Sometimes that's been clawing my way forward, wet and cold; other times sun-kissed with feelings of warmth that could only come from Jarrod's touch. Both are very real. The former I've come to associate with earthly separation; the latter, with heavenly closeness. The distance between these two points has grown shorter, but my hope, by God's grace, is to continue reducing the feeling of space between me and Jarrod. I am convinced that true closeness will only come on the day of our reunion in heaven.

I heard it often, that "time heals" or "you'll heal in time." For me, those words have always come from a place of love and kindness. Yet it is difficult to find words that can bring comfort to a parent's shattered heart after losing a child. What always came closest for me were hugs rather than words.

Even as I found myself on a path that revealed a new fire within me, I would still hear these words, almost as an echo or reaffirmation of the promises first spoken. I am careful now not to discourage anyone with the most fragile of hearts, so to be clear, time may heal. One thing I have learned, only from my own experience, is that we all grieve differently, and God may enter each of our lives differently. It would be foolish for me to presume my experience is transferable.

My intent here, early in our shared journey, is simply to explain my mindset. My hope is that something, maybe many things, within these pages will speak to your own heart.

This book is no endeavor in vanity, nor is it solely about honoring Jarrod. It has been driven by humility and by God's grace. If one story, lesson, or breakthrough of mine resonates with even a single person, that connection will warm my heart. And if that's you, consider me a trail companion for life, as perhaps our hearts have joined as a multiplied force of mutual comfort.

Let me also offer insight into why my vision is more about *healing* than about being *healed*. To me, being healed would mean a return to wholeness. As close as I have become with Jarrod in heaven, without him here on earth I cannot consider myself whole. My faith and hope remain unfaltering that this wholeness will come at the moment of our reunion in heaven. In that beautiful moment, I will not be parsing words for deeper meaning. I will be holding my son. At that embrace, I will be healed. Words, time, and space will likely be useless constructs in heaven anyway.

Until then, my journey is all about the meaning of those words, that time, and that space. Each can be arrows of strength or daggers of pain. All the miles I have walked in the wild places of God's creation, what I call "Heaven Hikes," have become a path of healing for me. The blessings along the way, the grace, mercy, and love, the presence of Jarrod and our closeness, have brought unimaginable seasons beyond mere survival. All of this has been healing for my heart, bringing me closer to peace.

If I could have seen and felt then what I see and feel now, I would not have been so critical when hearing "time will heal." I would have run for my boots and headed for the trail. What mattered most was not reaching the destination, but beginning the journey. I once discounted the power of healing simply because the thought of being healed felt impossible. Before I started, there was only separation.

Once I began walking, there was closeness. Both are measures of distance, but I chose to focus on how close I could be to Jarrod rather than despair over how far apart we were. I learned to count the steps upward, rather than count down the time.

It's in my nature to find irony or humor in most situations, often through dry wit or a gentle poke at myself.

But there is nothing to make light of in the grief I have felt and the path of suffering I have walked. My heartfelt respect extends to anyone living in this same "new reality," or loving someone who is. Jarrod had a way of making me smile, and our laughter together lifted me when days were hard. He did that when I had him here, and he continues to do that in how I hold him now. Any liberties I take in storytelling come from that same source of joy he gave me.

With this brief tee-up, please come along with me, on hikes, on walks down memory lane, and to today's vistas, as I share my vision for what comes next. What follows are not all detailed accounts of breathtaking summit views, but pieces of my journey, which I've often called an odyssey to give it the weight it deserves.

I've gathered bread crumbs from "Heaven Hikes" over these past fourteen years, truths that have enriched my personal path. My hope remains the same as I've shared earlier, that something here may be helpful to you. I wrestled with where to introduce these thoughts, up front, before the stories, or later, after their lessons unfolded. In the end, I chose a hiker's approach of offering a "trail map" for context before we begin. My intent is for you to have something to revisit and reflect on, whenever you feel moved to do so.

Before that, please accept my thanks. I am grateful that you are taking time to know Jarrod's story. Not nearly long enough, his eight years with us filled the pages of my heart, and the hearts of so many others. Thank you also for taking interest in my own continuing story as Jarrod's dad. Though still restless and suffering, I am able to feel joy again, to give and receive love again, and even to dream about the future.

Jarrod Kuhn, Sr.

BREAD CRUMBS
FROM HEAVEN HIKES:

Seeking Heaven

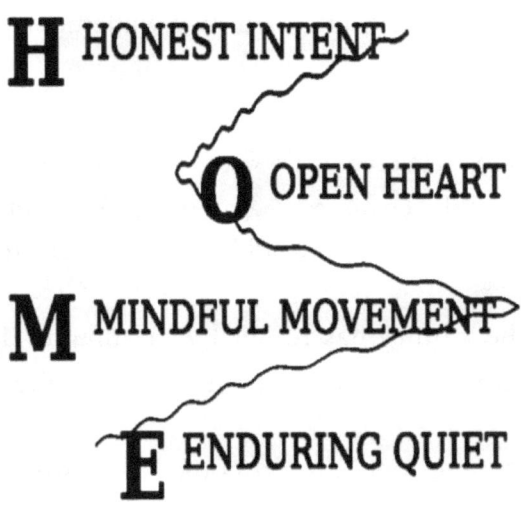

H HONEST INTENT

O OPEN HEART

M MINDFUL MOVEMENT

E ENDURING QUIET

Finding Home

GUIDING PURPOSE:

To embark on a journey of discovery, starting with honesty, then truly embracing openness, each step taken as a commitment to keep moving, in mindfulness, reaching out and accepting within, immersed in nature's heavenly closeness and renewal, a place of calmness and rest, as if arriving HOME.

STATEMENT OF HEART:

Born from grief, strengthened on the trail, and carried in faith, these principles reflect the lessons that reshaped my heart and restored meaning after the loss of my son.

They are offered not as answers, but as companions for those navigating their own wilderness.

1   Seeking Heaven isn't with an outstretched hand reaching toward the cosmos; it's an open heart reached within, what's underfoot and overhead helps the connection.

2   If the journey has reached a meaningful destination, it's in the form of a new beginning, not an end.

3   Sometimes the best gift comes from well-placed loneliness, and sometimes from well-timed loveliness, and sometimes from both.

4   Thoughts in the wild come when the mind's quiet, the heart's open, and there's enough pain in the legs to listen.

5   When the whisper of doubt creeps in, it's best to stay the course, remembering that the path met with resistance is usually the one worth keeping and defending.

6   Trails are more than switchbacks and pathways; they may be windows into hidden knowledge, when sensing beyond what meets the eye.

7   It's not height, distance or the climb in nature that unlocks truths; it's the courage to let go of the lies.

8   Trust in God means receiving blessings in answered prayers, and openness to accept grace in answered questions that hadn't been known to ask.

9   It's best to surrender in advance, before trying the matter on the trail, considering the outcome a gift, not grounds for appeal.

10   It's always a guest appearance in the wilderness, making oneself at home should come only after being graceful and gracious for the invitation, considerate of its wild nature, and taking care not to overstep.

HEAVEN HIKER'S PRAYER

Heavenly Father,

I lift my eyes to the hills,
and I find You there.
Maker of heaven and earth,
You steady my steps
and inspire me to keep moving.

In the quiet of the trail,
You open my heart
and still my mind.
In the shadow of grief,
Your light breaks through,
bringing clarity,
replacing lies with truth.

Keep my heart open,
my spirit honest,
my hope alive.
Bring me closer to You, Lord,
to Your kingdom.
In faith I draw strength,
knowing my child lives with You
in heaven.

Each stone, each tree, each breath
declares Your promise of rest and comfort.
In Your creation I find a home,
a restful mind, a peaceful heart.
You heal the brokenhearted

and proclaim Your eternal promise:
the end of suffering,
the joy of reunion,
the life everlasting to come.

In Jesus' name, Amen.

PART I
Reflections

1
STAY GOLD, PONY BOY

Even small children are known by their actions, so is their conduct really pure and upright.

—Proverbs 20:11

So, he got up and went to his father. But while he was a long way off, his father saw him and was filled with compassion for him; he ran to his son, threw his arms around him and kissed him.

—Luke 15:20

It is a wise father that knows his own child.

—William Shakespeare
(The Merchant of Venice)

Jarrod's heart touched so many. He was born an Angel from heaven, and for those who loved him in this world, he resumed that role far too soon. We only had him for eight years, yet in that short time, he changed the lives of everyone around him, his teachers, schoolmates, random strangers who thought they were playing *Call of Duty* with someone twice his age, his big sister Jillian, his aunts and uncles Jessica, Jacqueline, Chris, Tracy, Ian, and Jason, cousins Ethan and Emma, grandparents Rick and Suzanne, great-grandfather Ted. Even people who never met him, years later, would see pictures and be captivated by his smile.

CLASSIC JARROD

He was a gentle boy, never chasing popularity. Then again, it seemed the game always came to him. Playing tetherball alone before school, he caught the attention of someone who would become his best friend. One teacher was so struck by him that she nicknamed him Ponyboy, a nod to the sensitive, artistic, and intelligent kid from *The Outsiders*, the diamond in the rough.

His seemingly indifferent nature only made him more magnetic, especially to the girls. With his good looks and effortless style, Tony Hawk shirts, ripped jeans, slip-on Vans, and that early Bieber hair feathered over his ears, Valentine's cards carried more than hints of admiration.

His self-assured nature also found expression in his room, where he built whole worlds, imagination acted out, video games mastered, and Legos artfully created to reveal the depth of his curious mind.

His unassuming ways often felt like humility and grace beyond his years, beyond most years. I'm reminded of the time Jarrod scored so high on his state tests that he was invited to join GATE, the program designed to challenge students with exceptional academic talents. Jarrod was uninterested. His mom and I, of course, were proud, probably more than we let on, but it was classic Jarrod. He was modest, never chasing the spotlight, always content to let life find him. Only when he realized it would bring recognition to his school and classmates did Jarrod agree to participate. That was a signature Jarrod move.

It would be a mistake, though, to think his calm nature meant he wasn't adventurous. He pushed boundaries and took risks on the field and playground with a fearlessness that kept his mom and me constantly on edge.

Jarrod also had a sense of humor that caught people off guard. He was never the class clown, it wasn't his style, but every so often he'd slip into that role just long enough to make everyone laugh. That was his gift. He could be cool, calm, collected, and magnetic. Patient, deliberate, studious, and then suddenly spark the action. Humble, polite, and gracious, yet in the most unexpected ways, he could light up a room with laughter.

Jarrod carried skills, talents, and gifts that could have opened any door he chose later in life. I imagine him growing up to be the consummate gentleman, the friend who always showed up, someone around whom relationships formed easily and naturally.

His curiosity and determination had the potential to change the world he touched. I can see him falling deeply in love and becoming a devoted husband and father, steady in his care, generous with his attention, and fully present for the people who mattered most.

In just eight years, Jarrod gave us a glimpse of that perfect balance between a kind heart and a restless spirit.

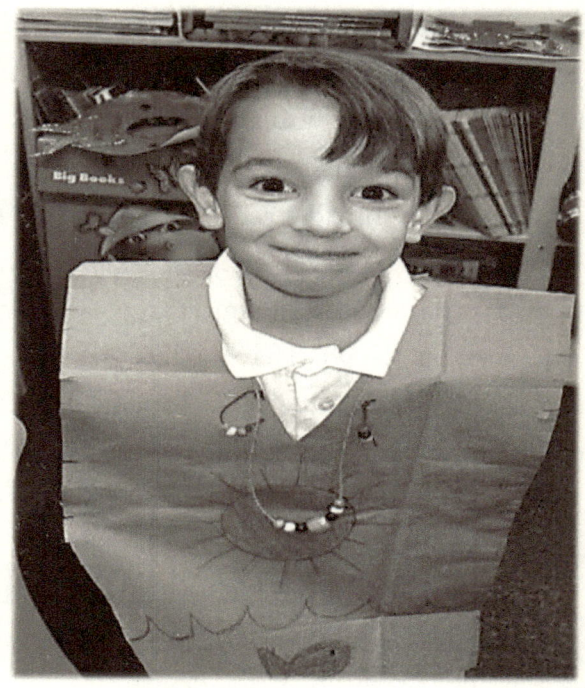

A HEART LIKE HIS

I can almost hear his conversation with God at the moment he realized Heaven was calling. His first thought would have been worry, voiced in the question: *What about my mom and dad?* God, I'm certain, would have reassured him that the reunion would come another day, not to worry. But knowing Jarrod, he would have pressed: *Until then, they'll be sad. And I'll miss them. Can't we come together later?* With a heart like Jarrod's, I am confident God would have answered, *I'll make sure they're cared for until it's their time.* I imagine only then would he have gone along willingly, not concerned for what he'd be missing out on, but for those who loved him and would feel in his absence.

2
LIGHT IN THE DARKNESS

Rejoice with those who rejoice; mourn with those who mourn.

—Romans 12:15

Praise be to the God and Father of our Lord Jesus Christ, the Father of compassion and the God of all comfort, who comforts us in all our troubles, so that we can comfort those in any trouble with the comfort we ourselves receive from God.

—2 Corinthians 1:3-4

Try to be a rainbow in someone's cloud.

—Maya Angelou
(Letter to My Daughter)

The outpouring of love we saw in the days following Jarrod's death was grace beyond anything I had ever known. It felt as though God had extended His hand over a small town and an unknown family, through acts of kindness when needed the most.

In those moments, we were living the words of Lamentations 3:22: *Because of the Lord's great love we are not consumed, for his compassions never fail.*

Our front door stayed open most days. It seemed easier than opening and closing it as often as someone knocked. People we didn't even know, far beyond our closest neighbors, came by with food, books, cards, and flowers. Most of the cards contained cash or checks, unsolicited generosity that humbled us. We were deeply grateful, especially since we were wholly unprepared for the expenses that suddenly flooded in.

I remember the priest who came to our house that first night. He sat in our family room for several hours, never saying a word. By then, the house was full of family and close friends, each trying to help us through the fog while carrying their own grief at losing Jarrod.

During the Funeral Mass later, the priest admitted he had been lost for words, but felt an undeniable pull to simply be present with us, moved by the sheer amount of love that filled the room.

One morning, very early, there was a knock at the door. It was a young girl, Jarrod's age, who had known him at school. In her hands was a small handful of picked flowers, which she shyly offered to Jarrod's mom and dad.

We had neighbors who were close friends, that stood by us now. Family flew in from across the country. Love and support surrounded us. Without it, I don't know how we would have eaten, made it out of bed, or functioned at all.

I had always loved the message of the poem *Footprints in the Sand*. Growing up, I remember seeing it on the wall. In those first days of grief, our minds drifted between denial, bargaining, and depression; anger would arrive soon enough.

Still, in those unpredictable days, I could see the footprints beside us, the reliable and firmly planted steps of family, faith, and friends walking with us when the ground felt weak. And in the hardest moments, when our strength gave out, I've come to believe those single tracks were when God Himself carried us part of the way.

FIELD OF ANGELS

Jarrod's elementary school, Tournament Hills, organized a full assembly in his honor. For many of the children, it was their first introduction to loss. Teachers, faculty, and students, the entire school, were grieving one of their own. The assembly was held on the field, the very place where Jarrod had played and laughed. In homage to his favorite baseball team, the children released red and white balloons as their way of saying goodbye.

He always chose the Angels on the field. Somehow, it feels right that he'd be one among them now.

Jarrod's mom, Jennifer, and I stood with the kids on the field, along with Jillian, participating, trying to show strength in the moment. We watched what seemed like hundreds of balloons lift into the sky and slowly disappear from sight. It was a mix of emotions that soon became our new normal, when every act of kindness or remembrance was inevitably followed by waves of grief and sorrow.

Jarrod's love for the Angels was no secret. His favorite teacher and her husband used their connections to arrange a moment of silence during a game, with Jarrod's picture displayed on the stadium screen of the Angels' minor league affiliate, the Inland Empire 66ers.

Even more moving was a personal act of kindness from an Angel himself, not just any player, but career Angel and World Series champion Tim Salmon. Word of Jarrod had reached him through the front office as we coordinated a small family outing. Jennifer and I had recently purchased a personalized brick in Jarrod's name, laid at the entrance to the stadium. It reads: *Jarrod Jr — Angel Forever.* We wanted to show it to loved ones and take in a game together in celebration of Jarrod.

A few days before the game, a box arrived from Tim Salmon. Inside was a signed World Series jersey. Jarrod had been a big fan of "King Fish," meeting him for an autograph signing a couple of years earlier. Holding that gift felt like one more example of God working through others to touch our hearts in ways we never could have imagined.

FACE OF GOD

Above all, there was one moment that left the most lasting impression on me. The cathedral was full during Jarrod's Funeral Mass, by my count, nearly three hundred people. The back doors stood open, and more were standing outside than there were pews inside.

It's not customary, but Father allowed personal testimony to be read at the altar. Jennifer and I couldn't bring ourselves to deliver the words, but a close family friend shared them on our behalf, offering what we hoped would breathe enduring life into Jarrod's wonderful spirit.

When the church service ended, we watched as Jarrod's casket was carried down the aisle, lifted into the hearse by strong men who loved him dearly. Jennifer and I walked slowly to our car for the drive to the graveside service. We had driven ourselves.

Just as we were about to get inside, a couple we had never met stepped forward and embraced us, first Jennifer, then me. Then another couple. And another. At first, I wasn't sure what was happening. Then I looked up toward the back doors of the church and saw it. A line of people, stretching as far as I could see, all coming forward for a hug.

What this felt like is impossible to capture in words. It was kindness beyond measure. It was unbridled love. I can only believe God knew Jennifer and I would need a depth of strength so profound that it would take an entire community to carry us forward, to the graveside, where we stood together as our eight-year-old boy was gently laid to rest.

The spiritual writer and teacher, Henri Nouwen, whose kindness has touched so many across the globe, reflected on his own lived experience of receiving unexpected acts of compassion. He said, "Community is the place where the person you least expect shows you the face of God."

As powerful as that warm embrace, that community hug, had been, and all the other acts of kindness that led up to it, those gestures only helped us survive the moment. In truth, nothing on earth could have lessened what came next.

The most heart-breaking sight a human eye can bear is watching the casket of a child lowered into the ground.

Jarrod's casket was graced with a spray of flowers, artfully arranged by the local florist and given as a gift, red and white roses encircling a baseball glove. By the time each person in attendance had placed a single rose of their own, Jarrod was covered in a garden of long-stemmed roses.

Yet even this beauty could not soften the echo of pain that rang out in a mother's cry at that final moment, a sound that opens a window into a heart so deeply wounded, into a bond so profound, it feels as though the soul itself has been torn apart.

3

WHOLE OF THE MOON

Although you see the world different than me—
Sometimes I can touch upon the wonders that you see—
And all the new colors and pictures you've designed.
Oh yes, sweet darling so glad you are a child of mine.

—Child of Mine
(Carole King)

The king was shaken. He went up to the room over the
gateway and wept. As he went, he said: "O my son Absalom!
My Son, my son Absalom! If only I had died instead of you—
O Absalom, my son, my son!

—2 Samuel 18:33

Jarrod's mom and I kept a short list of names for our boy on the way. Troy was a front runner. I'm sure that had nothing to do with my being a Cowboys fan, or with Troy Aikman leading three Super Bowl runs still fresh enough to replay in my mind. After some reflection, we chose something different.

THE NAME AND THE MIRROR

Not family tradition, not preordained. Just an idea at the time. We settled on a junior. The moment Jarrod was born I understood the deeper meaning. Looking into his eyes, I wasn't handing down a name. I was being handed a mirror. The gift I thought I was giving him was returned as something far greater, a reflection of myself I hadn't expected, one that would be immeasurable.

With his gentle heart and playful spirit, what was special about sharing our name was the joy that came from being Jarrod's dad. Every minute. Every day. For the eight precious years I'd have him on this earth. My name wasn't our only shared connection. There were countless others.

That same name, once a source of joy, would come back to haunt me in ways I could never have imagined. When the worst news a parent can receive became my horror story, it was our name in the headlines that struck me first. Memorials. School assembly announcements. Obituaries. In print, online, wherever it appeared. And how I would have traded places with him, taking back my name, owning those headlines alone, rewriting history so a young Troy could continue the life he so deserved.

16

PEANUTS AND CRACKER JACKS

Beyond the headlines, it was Jarrod's room that drew me in, a time capsule of mementos from our life together as father and son, preserved as if time itself had stopped. Inside his room it looked like our childhoods had overlapped, decades apart but stitched together into one perpetual story.

Star Wars action figures filled part of that story, my own young obsession, refreshed in his imagination. Sitting next to him I watched as lightsabers collided, rebellions sparked, empires toppled, galaxies rearranged in the space between his small hands. Amazing scenes unfolded before me.

At my age now I only saw plastic figures, but he saw whole new worlds. It reminded me of one of the '80s "new wave" favorites of my youth, the Waterboys' *Whole of the Moon*. The words now with a clarity I hadn't known until I watched Jarrod play:

> *I pictured a rainbow.*
> *You held it in your hands.*
> *I had flashes,*
> *but you saw the plan.*
> *I wandered out in the world for years,*
> *while you just stayed in your room.*
> *I saw the crescent.*
> *You saw the whole of the moon.*

Not all of our battles were imaginary. My own competitive encounters had once played out in bowling alleys. It wasn't a fad. It was an obsession. Picture a boy on a bike, bowling bag over the handlebars, pedaling toward the neighborhood lanes. Practice by day, funded by keeping score for the adult leagues at night. The dream was the PBA. Reality fell short, but better things awaited, like the day I bought Jarrod his first bowling ball.

After school, we'd go bowling. Jarrod picked it up fast. At six years old, he was hanging his heels off the back of the approach, charging the lane with a 5-step delivery that appeared choreographed, followed by a graceful release at the foul line. No bumpers for this young guy. He was throwing a hook with a ten-pounder, not like most kids his age, who used only two fingers in the ball, or none at all, the easy way to get it to turn down the lane. Jarrod, with the traditional grip, handled the ball with precision, lifting and rolling smooth as silk. Soon he was bowling in the 160s.

I saw his potential. Wait until he was sixteen and throwing fifteen pounds, I thought. Maybe he'd be the one to show up on a weekend broadcast of pro bowlers. There were afternoons when it felt like stepping into *Doc Brown's* time machine back to the '80s. If I looked into a mirror, I might have seen another kid bowling next to him, long bangs, a Depeche Mode shirt, corduroy Op shorts. We were more than father and son. We were best friends, hanging out after class.

It wasn't just the bowling ball. He took to the handlebars, too. Watching his cousin race BMX at Perris Raceway, he couldn't resist. One night, without warning, he grabbed a spare bike, checked into the next heat, and lined up at the gate. Shoulder to shoulder with seasoned riders, he launched down the drop, into a dirt track of jumps, turns, and the gauntlet. He braved it all, until one sharp turn sent him flying. Dust in his teeth, knees torn through his jeans, he climbed back up without a word, brushing off sympathy and pats on the back. He had faced the challenge, his first taste, and all he wanted now was a bike of his own.

He didn't know that my own boyhood joy was a hot-pink and white GT Performer. That I watched the movie *Rad* on repeat one summer. That I had once raced down the very same unforgiving run of dirt and dust he faced at Perris. But what we both knew, and shared without needing words, was the thrill of picking out his bike, a rite of passage from father to son.

The standout of all was a source of conflict with grandpa, a lifelong Dodgers fan. Despite his art of persuasion, and at times, outright bribery, Jarrod became, from day one, an Angels fan. I'll admit to nudging this one, but the choice was his to keep. Angels games became family outings. We'd also catch the Quakes, the Angels' early minor league step on the way to the Big Leagues. Jarrod even met Mike Trout, fresh to the roster, lucky enough to get his autograph while hanging over the fence near the bullpen.

This was yet another childhood parallel. Sitting next to Jarrod in the ballpark, me with a bag of peanuts and him with a box of Cracker Jacks, it easily transported me back to common ground. A boy so fascinated by his Angels that he'd get permission from his mom to stay home from school in 1986 to watch his team come one strike away from its first World Series appearance.

When the Angels did finally make it to the Series and win, it was just before Jarrod was born. When I shared all of the details of that hard-won, defining season with him it formed yet another special connection between us.

Years later, my Angel would be called home. His game only just beginning. Countless seasons left un-played. A field of dreams gone from view.

The Angels weren't the only family attraction in Anaheim. We were a Disney family, annual passholders and weekend warriors inside the park. Disneyland was another source of nostalgia and shared childhood experience. Growing up in Orange County, just a bike ride or bus stop from the park, it had been a long-known playground.

Along with our favorite rides, there was another passion that soon took on a life of its own. Every month, Disney released a new series of about five "Hidden Mickey" pins, available only from cast members. Collecting them meant trading any Disney pin, Hidden Mickey or not, with a cast member. Both traders and cast members wore their pins on lanyards.

Jarrod and his sister quickly became pros, and each month they managed to track down the full series, neatly arranged in a pin book for safekeeping. Mom and Dad got the leftovers, and even then, more often than not, we too managed to complete the sets.

I once overheard a rival pin-hunting family dub us the "Pin Sharks," a title I accepted as a *lanyard of honor.*
Apparently, we weren't just devoted. We were assertive. Admittedly, it wasn't a pastime for the faint of heart.

What really earned me the ability to weave blindly through the crowds, though, was my time as a cast member, one of my first jobs as a teenager. Passing on those moves and bits of insider savvy no doubt helped shape my baby Pin Sharks. Jarrod was especially impressed with one pin in particular. My anniversary pin, the one I wore proudly on my lanyard. In time, it found its way to his, another heartfelt handoff from father to son.

SANCTUARY AND SPRINKLERS

After losing Jarrod, his bedroom became my sanctuary. The memories there weren't neatly organized. It was, after all, an eight-year-old boy's room. Inside, though, a treasure trove and timeworn bounty. The colorful swirl of a bowling ball, a mini-helmet signed by former Angels player Bobby Grich, shoeboxes of Star Wars figures, the red BMX bike we convinced a state champ to sell us.

However, most captivating of all were the unfinished Legos, silent testaments to his imagination. Many nights I sat with those bricks, trying to piece together what I thought he'd build. I could assemble the pieces but not the magic.

That was the point. Despite all we shared, Jarrod was one of a kind. I don't remember the exact moment it came back to me, only that it did. Fatherhood was never about cloning myself. It was about charting a course for my son, who might resemble me and yet grow beyond me in ways I could never anticipate. Looking back, that was when the

Whole of the Moon

responsibility and the reverence of fatherhood came into focus.

Although Jarrod's room was a place of solitude and remembrance, it was rarely a resting place. Many nights didn't end with peaceful reflection, or even without some drama outside the house. At times, grief so heavy dragged me to the dark side.

Jarrod's grave sat half a mile from our home and his beloved elementary school. During some raw periods of loss, I'd find myself there at night. At first, just shooting the breeze with my son, catching him up on how the Angels were doing, stories about his sister, movies he'd like.

Before long, the conversations turned elsewhere. Anger at God. Tears I couldn't stop. Hands clutched around the picture of Jarrod smiling on his headstone, holding on as if I could really feel him.

Several hours later, the sunrise would usher in another day. It was joined by the sprinklers, and the realization that I had spent the night. Another morning, waking up wet and exhausted.

PART II
Seeking Heaven

4

SHIFTING GEARS

God, grant me the serenity to accept the things I cannot change, courage to change the things I can, and the wisdom to know the difference.

—Reinhold Niebuhr

There is a time for everything, and a season for every activity under the heavens.

—Ecclesiastics 3:1

He lifted me out of the slimy pit, out of the mud and mire; he set my feet on a rock and gave me a firm place to stand.

—Psalm 40:2

By this time, the world had long settled back into its normal cadence, seemingly leaving me in the dust. Friends and family who had once been semi-permanent houseguests in the days and weeks after losing Jarrod had returned to their own routines. It's surreal how this dynamic unfolds.

One moment the refrigerator is full of meals, lovingly delivered by neighbors, coworkers, friends, and family. Each and every kindness received as gracious and appreciated. The house is alive with voices and footsteps. And then, almost abruptly, the support recedes. Understandably so. In truth, at the time, it may have even been welcome, a breath of normalcy, the thought of such anyway. For a bereaved parent, though, the hard truth is normal is long gone. The new reality is foreign, unrecognizable.

For me, that void often stirred a restless energy, a feeling that I needed to take on the world, to make Jarrod's name echo in meaningful ways.

In the spirit of Emily Dickinson's poem "Unable are the loved to die," I would be consumed with thoughts on how to keep Jarrod's name alive, refusing to let the love for him fade.

Some days, that fire burned bright; other days, it collapsed into another "sprinkler sunrise." Sometimes I'd spend whole weekends in bed, paralyzed.

Grief came in many forms. Rage that shouted blame, sorrow that whispered shame, silence that confirmed life would never be the same. Each one with a different face of pain, arriving unannounced, weighted differently, but unrelenting nevertheless.

SEPARATE GRIEFS

The house wasn't only silent and motionless after the departure of well-wishers, the same hands that had quite literally carried us through the first several months of pain and suffering.

These were desperate times, a depth of anguish beyond anything we had known. John Milton said it best, "The mind is its own place, and in itself can make a heaven of hell, a hell of heaven."

Jennifer and I had once been blessed with young love, a story visibly told through high school prom pictures, shared college textbooks, snapshots from a Disney-inspired wedding, and photo albums filled with us cradling two precious babies. Our story could have played out like a John Hughes film, part *Ferris Bueller's Day Off* and *The Breakfast Club* from my end, joined with Jennifer's *Some Kind of Wonderful*.

It was from the strength of this love, nurtured and reinforced over more than two decades, that the foundation of our family was built. Weekends at Disneyland with a rented green stroller, our name card reading simply "Kuhn Family," seemed to say it all. Everything was going according to plan. Not without course corrections. Those were constant. But we navigated the detours together, often turning them into bridges toward something better.

We shared so much in common, and the playful spirit that first drew us together in youth carried forward through the years. Jennifer's family had become more mine than my own. With her sisters, Jessica and Jacqueline, and their husbands, Ian and Jason, our gatherings resembled the light-hearted but meaningful moments of a sitcom coffee shop, more best friends than in-laws.

Her dad, Rick, my Godfather, was much more than a title. He and I would spend hours, often without fanfare from our wives, listening to music and shooting pool until morning. Those were special sunrises. Her mom, Suzanne, is a beautiful spirit, whose patience, kindness, and generosity of heart seemed effortless. When I lost my own mother in my twenties, just a few years after Jennifer and I were married, it was Suzanne who stepped in and helped me beyond measure.

Despite our bond and shared history, losing Jarrod proved too much. John Lennon's aspirational line, "all you need is love," has its limits. For reasons impossible to fully explain, ours were reached. As strong as that foundation had once been, the building blocks of our home and family could not withstand the storm that followed Jarrod's death. Some forces are simply too strong.

Robert Frost lost his beloved son, Elliott, at age three. Years later, he wrote *Home Burial*. In the poem, a husband and wife stand at opposite ends of the same grief, speaking past each other. His need to speak the loss and her refusal to hear it is central to how differently sorrow can be felt and lived. A husband and wife unable to share grief, the distance between them widening with every word left unsaid.

At its heartbeat, the poem reveals irreconcilable and inconsolable differences in how grief can befall a mother and father, wife and husband. She needs empathy he can't voice, and his desperation to connect through reason she can't bear.

The following excerpt of the dialogue in *Home Burial* feels reminiscent to me:

He: *What is it you see from up there always—for I want to know.*

She: *[Silent]*

He: *What is it you see... I will find out now—you will tell me, dear.*

She: *[Still refuses]*

He: *Oh, Oh...*

She: *What is it—what?*

He: *Just that I see.*

She: *You don't. Tell me what it is.*

He: *The wonder is I didn't see at once. I never noticed it from here before...the little graveyard where my people are! ... so small the window frames the whole of it ... there are three stones of slate and one of marble ... broad-shouldered little slabs in the sunlight ... But I understand: it is not the stones, but the child's mound—*

She: *Don't, don't, don't, don't!*

He: *Can't a man speak of his own child he's lost?*

She: *Not you! ... I must get out of here. I don't rightly know that any man can.*

He: *Don't go to someone else this time. Listen to me... there's something I'd like to ask you, dear.*

She: *You don't know how to ask it.*

He: *Help me, then… my words are nearly always an offense. I don't know how to speak of anything so as to please you… let me into your grief… give me my chance… What was it… to take your mother-loss of a… child so inconsolably—in the face of love. You make me angry… and it's come to this… A man can't speak of his own child that's dead.*

She: *You can't because you don't know how to speak…the heart's gone out of it: why keep it up… you think the talk is all… I must go— somewhere out of this house.*

My entire life had been defined by roles: Jennifer's boyfriend, then husband, later a dad, and always intent on being the provider and protector. Then, as if waking from a nightmare you hope ends in a cold sweat of relief, I found myself living it all the same. An empty house. Single. Part-time dad. Lost in compounded grief. The shadows of another life, lived not so long ago, trailed me everywhere.

What remained were three mixed-breed chihuahuas, Kenobi, Chewy, and Luke, rescued by Jarrod and Jillian and left in my care, a responsibility I hadn't expected in a life already changed.

QUIET IN THE HELMET

After a while, the "sprinkler sunrises" came less often. Grief was still there, raw and deliberate at times, but the ambushes grew less constant, like a thief that visited in the night, though less frequently now.

One thing that helped, oddly enough, was riding my bike. Strange, maybe, but it centered me. Years earlier I had been a cyclist, not competitive, just a century rider. Then life shifted. Work grew busy, weekends became family time, and the bike hung untouched in the garage.

However, grief has a way of revealing truths. I learned quickly that sitting still, whether in bed, on the couch, or bellied up to a bar, each could lead me back to another sprinkler sunrise. Keep moving, I told myself. What better way to keep moving than keep pedaling?

What I discovered was that motion helped. Routines, kept with discipline, centered me. Beyond work, that meant climbing onto my bike, every day.

At 25, Theodore Roosevelt lost his mother, Martha, to Typhoid fever, and on the same afternoon, in the same house, lost his wife, Alice, to kidney disease, just two days after giving birth to their daughter. Overcome with grief, the date was marked with an "X" in his personal diary, along with the words, "the light has gone out in my life." He'd later come to realize that darkness had less a chance of keeping up with a man on the move, revealed by his later journal entry, "black care rarely sits behind a rider whose pace is fast enough."

From there, hopeful to outpace his grief, Roosevelt charted a new course, to the Dakota Territory, seeking the active life of a cowboy and sanctuary in nature. Seventeen years later, he'd become President of the United States and from that office gave back to the wilderness he dearly loved, conserving vast amounts as healing grounds for future generations. It would appear that in time he'd found some measure of *new light in his life.*

For me, I peddled faster and faster, not running from the realities that were the sources of my grief. It was merely an effort to get in front of its dreadful pull toward misery. Inside my helmet, there was a rare calmness. The clutter of grief began to give way to focus, ideas clear of noise, thoughts before triggers. Soon I found myself looking forward to those rides, counting down the hours until the day gave way to the road. As a bonus, the miles brought their own rewards. I lost weight, grew stronger, and found myself tackling longer rides, even climbing hills I once would have avoided.

For that next year, the bike became my refuge, an escape hatch that carried me to a place where my mind could finally grow quiet enough to think.

On one of those rides, a thought surfaced. Another love I had long abandoned. Hiking. Memories stirred of trails walked with Jarrod at Zion, Bryce, and other parks. He was young then, perched in a carrier on my back. In retrospect, it was less a hike and more a pleasure cruise, for him. For me, it was a joy. I happily carried him, not realizing then how special those moments really were and what I'd give years later for just one more.

God and I still had a contentious relationship. From my side, it was mostly cursing, lamenting, and blaming. Yet even through that anger, I felt a gentle pull to open my Bible. Doing so became the start of a journey, a rediscovery. A quest for answers. A longing for understanding. My heart, though terribly wounded, was opening to the possibility of new purpose.

I was being reminded of one of my favorite poems by Maykov, *Don't Say*:

> *Don't say that there is no escape,*
> *and that your troubles wear you out.*
> *The darker the night, the brighter the stars.*
> *The deeper the sorrow, the closer to God.*

I didn't plan it, but I began at the beginning, the Book of Genesis. The creation story drew me in. At times it stirred wonder, other times it brought tears. And then came a eureka moment. Heaven and Earth; this was the distance between me and Jarrod. Earth, I knew all too well. Heaven, not so much.

In my heart, I believed Heaven was where my son was. I found reassurance in the words of Matthew 19:14, where Jesus told his disciples, *Let the little children come to me, and do not hinder them, for the kingdom of heaven belongs to such as these.*

How, then, could I draw closer to Heaven, I wondered? The clarity I found on the bike had already shown me how motion could quiet the noise. But what about elevation? What would my mind feel on a mountaintop, in the clouds? Would I be close enough to hear a whisper? Could Jarrod reach out to me through nature?

At first, it was only a thought. Then the thought became a calling, one I couldn't ignore.

The words of Matthew 11:28–29 stirred a new hope in me, God's priceless invitation: *Come to me, all you who are weary and burdened, and I will give you rest. Take my yoke upon you and learn from me, for I am gentle and humble in heart, and you will find rest for your souls.*

It felt like a call to step away from sprinkler sunrises and toward something drier, more hopeful, and filled with promise. C. S. Lewis writes in *A Grief Observed*, reaching a transitional point in his own grief, that "you can't see anything properly while your eyes are blurred with tears."

It was time to surrender, open and dry my eyes. To rest in what I could understand, to trust what was held in God's greater plan, and to see even the unanswerable questions as a form of grace. In time, with courage, they might shape the wisdom to know the difference.

So where does one go when newly inspired? Naturally, Google. I wasn't after a grand challenge, just a walk in nature to see what might show up. Unwittingly, I clicked my way into a website that dared hikers to take on the *Six Pack of Peaks*.

A DIFFERENT SIX PACK

The *Six Pack* of Peaks had a nice ring to it. I wasn't a stranger to six packs. Beer, of course. Not proud to admit it, but in those first months after losing Jarrod, numbing myself that way had been too common a crutch. More recently, thanks to the bike, there was even the faint outline of a different six pack forming above the waistline. So why not?

The challenge, organized by *SoCal Hiker*, was a self-paced series of treks across Southern California's ranges. No race, no medals, just the mountains, the trail, and whoever committed to take them on. Perfect for me. I wasn't ready yet for group outings. My motivation was more meditative than meetup. The format fit just right, pointing me to an inflection point and trailheads I hadn't known I was seeking.

In Homer's terms, I had stumbled onto more than a journey. For me, it had the makings of an *odyssey*, trails and trials, not just miles.

What I was looking forward to wasn't a stroll through a city park. These climbs were in rugged terrain demanding respect. Non-technical, thankfully, no ice axes or crampons on my REI shopping list. Maybe that would come later, I thought. For now, certainly ambitious enough and a fitting challenge. What did make the list were boots, trekking poles, and the nudge within to keep moving.

The *Six Pack* of Peaks challenge started modestly in the San Gabriels above LA. Then, the hikes escalated, climbing higher, becoming harder, and taking longer, through the San Bernardino and San Jacinto ranges. The opener was Mt. Wilson, 5,700 feet, with its landing spot at the famed observatory, once home to the world's largest telescope. The finale, Old Grayback, rose above 11,500 feet, the highest point in Southern California, its broad summit visibly gray from the weight of weather and years standing tall.

First stop, though, was REI. Shopping for gear is half the fun of pretending you know what you're doing. With help from the experts in the store, I walked out with a pair of Salomon Quest boots, carbon fiber poles, a three-liter CamelBak, and a lighter wallet. Here's to commitment, I thought, filling my trunk, emptying my bank account, and daring heaven to join me for the climbs ahead.

Training began with long day hikes in the desert and high country, Idyllwild, Joshua Tree and Palm Springs foothills. I was prepping for ten to seventeen miles in a single day, with vertical gains of four to six thousand feet. Every trail was its own training-ground, every climb a reminder that cycling didn't automatically translate to hiking fitness.

Still, each mile worked the muscles and built the confidence. Combined with discipline to keep at it, I was well on my way. There were those who were worried about this adventure I was about to embark on, apprehensions of me becoming hopelessly lost in the wilderness. Jarrod's sister, Jillian, being one of them. Fortunately, all of these trails were heavily trafficked. Dozens of strangers snaking their way up switchbacks, strung out across ridges, each in their own private universe of thirst, pain and discovery, probably in that order.

Yosemite Park Ranger Shelton Johnson once wrote in his book *Gloryland* that "all you need to get to Heaven is a good pair of boots." With inspiration like that, I felt ready. By March, I had fully embraced the challenge, choosing to take the hikes in order, each peak preparing me for the next. Mt. Wilson was first in my crosshairs.

Geared up, and standing at the base with my backpack cinched tight, I looked back once, checking straps, settling nerves, and giving a silent nod to the passenger I imagined riding along.

It was as if Jarrod Jr. leaned close, that eager tap on my shoulder, the same one I knew so well whenever an adventure was about to begin, his voice clear as ever:

"Let's go, Dad!"

5
PATH SET IN LIGHT

In every walk with nature, one receives far more than he seeks.

—John Muir
(Steep Trails)

You will go out in joy and be led forth in peace; the mountains and hills will burst into song before you, and all the trees of the field will clap their hands.

—Isaiah 55:12

God saw all that he had made, and it was very good....

—Genesis 1:31

Only a mile into the fourteen that is the Mt. Wilson hike, less than an hour on the trail, I took a short detour to Sturtevant Falls, which was flowing beautifully. Rising about fifty feet inside a canyon lined with sycamores and oaks, water roared down a veil of green moss and rock into a creek below.

I was already in awe, standing in the cool, misty breeze. It felt worth pausing for reflection. Psalm 42:7 comes to mind: *Deep calls to deep in the roar of your waterfalls; all your waves and breakers have swept over me.*

To me, those words are a hopeful call for God's mercy when grief threatens to pull you under. Certainly, the force of a waterfall is proof enough of creation's might. Detour or not, I felt on course, searching for deeper meaning in the heart of nature.

Back on the main trail, I pressed forward, leaving behind the creek-side path for switchbacks that revealed steeper steps ahead. Not far from the trail stood curious old cabins, relics of the early 1900s. Four miles in I reached Sturtevant Camp, the perfect spot for lunch. Nothing special packed, a simple PB&J and some tangerines.

I sat at a picnic bench beneath the shade of a cedar, where I pulled a small journal out of my pack, a place to jot down trail details, discoveries, or anything that surfaced in silence. Someday this notebook, I hoped, would contain a trail map to heavenly closeness.

As I ate, I was joined by a Steller's Jay, probably with an eye on some future bread crumbs from my sandwich. Its vivid blue colors were striking. It hopped and chattered through the branches above, occasionally darting from cedar limb to forest floor, foraging, filling the canyon with sounds that ranged from laughter to resembling a crow's rougher call.

I sat mesmerized until my food was gone. Refueled, I packed up, nodded to my feathered companion, a few crumbs left behind, and set back on the trail.

FEARLESS AS A CHILD

The remaining miles wound steadily upward. Somewhere along the switchbacks I came upon a buzz of honeybees. That sound, that moment, carried me back to Jarrod. When he was little, we lived in a townhouse with a round drain cover near the front door.

On one hot afternoon, wasps gathered on it, an apparent cooler spot to escape the heat and gather water. Jarrod, maybe six, crouched beside it with a mason jar and lid in hand. Each time a wasp landed, he scooped it in and snapped the lid shut. Another landed, in it went. With a filled jar of furious wasps, he walked inside proud to show both of us his accomplishment.

I was stunned. How had he done it without a single sting, overcome that one clever wasp smarter than the rest with a better survival instinct? The skill, the care it must have taken to pop the lid open for a new catch without letting the others escape.

I was impressed. His mother was not. In fact, compared to her reaction, the wasps were tame. Somehow, I was guilty by proximity, deemed an accomplice. My new assignment was to help facilitate the release of the wasps. Knowing I lacked Jarrod's still hands, we struck a deal. He'd pop the lid. I'd run like hell.

The plan worked. That was Jarrod, fearless, surprising me with talents I never saw coming. It reminds me now of Matthew 18:3, when Jesus said, *Truly I tell you, unless you change and become like little children, you will never enter the kingdom of heaven.*

Watching Jarrod that day, with his calm confidence and unshaken spirit, I saw what childlike faith and courage really looked like.

EARTHLY VIEWS, COSMIC LENS

As the switchbacks tightened and the canyon widened behind me, the sound of the creek faded into nothing but my own huffing and puffing, the sun pressing down harder with each step. The last miles were the cruelest, nearly two thousand feet of vertical grind in just three miles.

I caught a glimpse of Mt. Baldy through the trees, a reminder of even higher climbs to come. A squirrel darted across the trail, pausing just long enough to glance back, as if to question whether I'd make it. I stopped too, draining my CamelBak deeper than at any other point, willing myself onward through heat and fatigue.

And then, almost suddenly, the trail spilled out into something unexpected. It wasn't a rugged summit, but the carefully laid grounds of the Mt. Wilson Observatory. I had made it. Inside the largest dome, a few steps away now, stood the famed 100-inch Hooker Telescope. The instrument that offered an expanded vision of the cosmos, proving that the Milky Way was not the universe but only an island in an ocean of galaxies stretching millions of light years across.

Around the corner was the Cosmic Café, a rare treat atop a mountain. I ordered the "Hiker's Special," a hot dog, soda, and cookie. Minutes later, the voice at the window called out: "One Hiker's Special for a special hiker named Jarrod." The words, gift-wrapped in coincidence and grace.

I savored every bite, enjoying the views over the LA basin, that stretched from the skyline to the coast. The descent came easier, a different trail leading back to the same lot where I'd parked.

This hike raised thoughts of St. Francis of Assisi, a devout steward of creation, who called nature the "mirror of God." On the trail, I found my reflection in that mirror, pine and eucalyptus in the air, water flowing with purpose, bluebirds telling stories from the branches.

Juxtaposed with this living scene was another kind of mirror, the 100-inch glass at Mt. Wilson, gathering light in ways our own eyes could only dream of. A literal mirror in time, reflecting the immensity of creation itself.

How fitting that my first climb, meant to reach toward heaven, brought me to the very lens that had revealed just how vast creation is.

My legs ached, but my heart was full. I ended this hike more inspired than ever to continue the journey of discovery. I had felt Jarrod throughout the day, in the memories that surfaced, in the gentle breeze that seemed shared, and it brought me peace.

My first summit left me hungry for more. Next up was Cucamonga Peak. I'd have to wait a couple of weeks, filling the time with local hikes to keep my legs fresh, my spirit ready, and my eyes lifted toward the next horizon.

GUIDED BY THE LORD'S CANDLE

I arrived about 7 a.m. Saturday morning at the Icehouse Canyon Trailhead. Today's hike would be roughly fourteen miles out and back, with 4,300 feet of vertical gain. I was greeted again by that defining scent of pine from a couple of weeks earlier. Adventure Pass on the dash, I laced up my boots and slung the pack on, poles already cinched to the back.

Like pranayama, the breathing techniques used to calm the spirit and ease the mind before meditation, this ritual of changing into my hiking gear was both transitional and transformative. When the boots were on, I unplugged from all that was behind me, focusing only on what lay ahead. In the proper mental state, what stretched before me was an uneven trail of dirt and river rock.

I'd walked about two miles along a running creek, lined with ferns, moss, and tall grass, passing the remains of cabins now long abandoned. The trail soon narrowed into a section of granite slabs and required occasional scrambling across broken stone. Serenity had already settled in. The early sounds of nature stirred around me, but otherwise it was the silent paradise I longed for.

My mind was opening up. Back at the creek, a yucca plant had caught my eye. Symmetrical balls of green arrows pointed in every direction. Some bore a tall stalk rising from the center with a white bloom at its crown. Early Catholic settlers affectionately called it *Vela de Nuestro Señor*— "Our Lord's Candle"—leaning into that white bloom for its warm glow and subtle offering of wild ambiance, a curious spring of color brightening its barren surroundings. It was a recognition of God's presence in wild places.

The yucca was not only a sentinel standing tall but also a giver of creation, its fibers woven into sandals and baskets, its stalk roasted for food, its roots ground for soap and medicine. Revered, practical, and beautiful, it embodied both survival and spirit.

Soon I reached an outcropping, the saddle, as it's called, where several trail junctions converged. It was a place to pay attention. I was deep in the backcountry now, Jillian's voice in my head reminding me not to get hopelessly lost in the wilderness. Trail signs pointed the way to Ontario Peak, the Three Ts, or my intended path toward Cucamonga Peak. It felt like nature's own rebranding of those "Choose Your Own Adventure" books we all loved in the '80s.

One of the Three Ts was Thunder Mountain, which for a fleeting moment tempted me toward a detour. It was a nod to Jarrod's and my favorite ride at Disneyland. But reason won out. Jillian's regular presence was with me, tapping my shoulder, guiding me to stay the course. Ahead rose the mountain itself, seemingly out of reach, its slopes lush with fir and pine stretching as far as the eye could see. I pressed on toward the base of the switchbacks. One step at a time.

SUN KISSES AND SON'S HUGS

Grinding upward, the mountain opened to broader horizons, rolling ridgelines unfurling into the distance. Then came something I hadn't expected, an experience that would capture my curiosity for years. It felt as though a sunbeam had settled directly on my face. The heat of the day was strong, but this was different. The air around me seemed to settle, holding a warm kiss of light, just long enough to pull my thoughts away from the dusty trail. Later I would learn it was likely a thermal pocket, common in mountain ridges where uneven heating of the air creates sudden pockets of still, concentrated warmth.

Whether a heavenly sun-kiss or a scientific phenomenon, it carried me straight into thoughts of Jarrod. The memory that surfaced was of his JanSport backpack. It began with one, then a couple, but eventually all fifteen numbered pool balls dangled from the bottom, intended as keychains, but repurposed into a tribute to one of his favorite games.

They doubled as an early-warning system, clinking together in a chained melody to announce Jarrod's arrival long before he was seen. Sometimes it was me picking him up from school. Bless his heart, Jarrod would run toward me, the rattling backpack sounding like a parade rolling through. It was music to my ears, and when his arms wrapped around me, I knew I had all I needed in this world.

One JanSport memory in particular came rushing back as I pushed painfully up the switchbacks. I had taken a day off work and was in the backyard planting a small sego palm, no taller than ten inches. Jennifer had picked Jarrod up from school, and while I was lost in my task, he came barreling through the slider, backpack still on, keychains clattering in symphony.

He ran straight to me and wrapped me in a hug. In that moment, I knew how lucky I was to be his dad, and how proud I was of his kind nature. Looking back now, those hugs were *my* Lord's Candle, Jarrod's light, shining when I needed it most. When I close my eyes today and listen for those keychain melodies, I can still feel those special hugs.

Farther up the switchbacks, I convinced myself that the warmth felt was his embrace. In the words of Buddhist teacher Jack Kornfield, "if you wish to know the divine, feel the wind on your face and the warm sun on your hand." I dared the science to prove me wrong. In that regard, even Albert Einstein once wrote, "The most beautiful thing we can experience is the mysterious." There it was, I thought, suggestions hinting at support by the Father of Relativity himself.

I finally crossed the last crest, the switchbacks giving way to a steep walk toward the summit, across scattered pine needles and loose gravel. At last, I stood on my second peak. The elevation, 8,900 feet, offered views stretching across the Inland Empire and, on this clear day, all the way to Catalina Island.

The summit itself jutted forward in the shape of a diving-board, an outstretched boulder seemingly forged into the mountaintop. The more daring hikers stepped onto this natural plank for their summit photo, or sat near its edge with legs dangling over. My picture was less bold, but to me, glorious all the same.

SILENT TESTIMONY AND GUARDIANS

I hadn't eaten much on the way up, just a few tangerines and Clif Bars. The saddle might have worked for a lunch stop, but with good momentum I had pressed on. Now the peak was the perfect place for rest and a snack before the descent.

Seated on a rock, I turned from the sweeping skyward view back toward the mountain itself. On the final approach I had already noticed them, but now curiosity overtook me. The trees. They looked almost fossilized, remnants that seemed long gone yet somehow still clung to the mountain, tethered in stubborn silence.

At first glance, they could be dismissed as lifeless husks. But their twisted forms told stories. Roots that once anchored them still held a lasting connection. Their weathered scars bore witness to forces endured, wind, snow, heat, and time itself. Like elders of the forest, they carried legacies beyond their thriving years, windows into their struggle to survive.

Of all the memories I would recall of Jarrod on this journey, there were also moments when I found myself enthralled by nature's own memories. These skeletal trees, as timeless as the mountain itself, lived on in their absence. They told stories not only of survival, but of endurance, and left an impression as lasting as the summit beneath my feet.

The afternoon was wearing on, and a deeper study of those trees would have to wait. I'd be back. For now, it was time to hustle. Nobody wants to come off a trail after dark, especially without a headlamp. Acquainted now with the way back, and still carrying the spring in my step from bagging peak number two, I moved quickly. At times it was a fast walk, at others a light jog. I slowed only after reaching the saddle, careful to make the proper turn again. Soon I was back on the narrow passage, hemmed in by those same rocky slabs stacked one atop another.

The heat of the day had worn me down. My legs and feet were close to surrender. My thoughts drifted, lost in memory and imagination. I was aware of my surroundings, but only in the periphery. That would change in an instant. Halfway through the slabs, I heard a rattle, like thunder in stone. My eyes snapped to the sound as if pulled by instinct. There, wedged between two slabs, was a large diamondback, coiled tight. No distant shadow, this was up close and personal. We locked in on each other. I had brushed against the far side of the path, startling him, and he responded in kind.

The encounter was brief, more about respect than threat. A reminder that hiking is always a guest appearance in the wild, never a right of way. The diamondback wasn't out

Heaven Hikes

53

to harm me. He was simply saying, watch your step. Or, depending on his mood, perhaps channeling Clint Eastwood, with a bit grumpier, "get off my lawn." Either way, the message landed. From that point forward, I was no longer in my head. My focus turned steely, fixed on every inch of trail until I made it safely back.

Going higher and farther this time, I had collected another of the six peaks. Unlike Wilson, this summit offered its own mirror in time, not through the lens of a telescope, but in the weathered trees that stood as nature's reflection, spanning past to present.

With enough silence and stillness, even in motion, the distance between me and Jarrod felt shorter. Precious memories of his hugs, and the very real-feeling kiss on the cheek, lingered as the moment that would stay with me the longest.

I was reminded by the promise of Psalm 126:5, *those who sow with tears will reap with songs of joy*. The trail made the promise feel less distant, one step at a time.

I was starting to feel God's touches in his world of creation, windows into nature's beauty and closeness to Jarrod. I was hopeful that the momentum would continue to build, in the form of deeper faith and further blessings.

I had also made a new discovery, one of God's gems in creation, the aptly named Lord's Candle. The next hike would wait a couple of weeks. This time, the path would climb even higher and farther. Mt. Baldy, the last of the San Gabriels on the list, a peak I had already glimpsed from the first two summits. For now, though, my mind turned toward home. Hot water. A good soak in the jacuzzi.

6
FOUR SAINTS, DEVIL'S BACKBONE

You will seek me and find me when you seek me with all your heart.

—Jeremiah 29:13

No temptation has overtaken you except what is common to mankind. And God is faithful; he will not let you be tempted beyond what you can bear. But when you are tempted, he will also provide a way out so that you can endure it.

—1 Corinthians 10:13

The mind, once stretched to a new idea, never returns to its original dimensions.

—Ralph Waldo Emerson
(Nature)

Virgil, in the *Aeneid*, refers to the following words as a call to courage and destiny:

SIC ITUR AD ASTRA
Thus one goes to the stars.

In time, the phrase became a motto adopted by military regiments and universities, urging men and women alike to reach higher and achieve more. I knew the story, and the motto, broadly speaking. It had the ring of something I wanted to claim as my own marching order for the trail. Yet, it wasn't perfect.

The Stoic philosopher, Seneca, struck closer to my heart, with the words:

NON EST AD ASTRA MOLLIS E TERRIS VIA
There is no easy way from the earth to the stars.

This landed truer. Needless to say, I was probing words and questioning insights of ancient artists and teachers celebrated thousands of years beyond their lives. No apologies. I wanted something that felt true to me, as a call to action.

This was about finding renewed intimacy with *my* timeless treasure, and personal quest to find closeness with places otherworldly. All considered, it wasn't scholarly as it was engaging and thoughtful. My intent was to unearth whatever wisdom I could, from any source that came across authentic, aligned with my purpose, that would imprint on my heart. I was guided by some familiarity with Latin from law school, but by no means any authority from a lens of expert in literature, philosophy or theology.

However, I was hopeful that the Holy Spirit would guide me. Ultimately, I reached the promise land, so to speak, with the discovery of George Whitefield. An 18th Century evangelical, he had fashioned a personal seal that bore a winged heart rising above the globe with the motto:

ASTRA PETAMUS
Let us seek the stars (*Heaven*).

So, it wasn't in the form of ancient wisdom, either considered sage advice or best practice, that rang true. It was a modern revivalist's own intimate calling that stirred me. Open mind and heart at this point. My intent off the trail was a thirst for earthy meaning, so that my time on the trail would be focused on heavenly feeling.

It might seem trivial to spend the time and energy on such an exercise, though what pushed me past that criticism, which certainly came to my own mind, was a reminder of those two words that would govern all else: KEEP MOVING.

Off the trail, this meant reading, learning, reflecting, and yes, even choosing mottos. I don't need to say this to a bereaved parent; sleepless nights are already understood. For others who love someone grieving, that reality may be less apparent.

Sometimes, being restless was actually not as terrible as it sounds. It too, in its own way, could be tranquil. As peaceful as the trail can be, and how powerful a sanctuary it did become personally, nighttime is a doorway into another world. One of the realities, the new normal as we sometimes refer to it, is that time is measured differently.

Those days of being in sync, when my wristwatch kept time simply through motion, had largely slipped away. This was now a time of self-winding. However, I was determined that the time would not go to waste. That it'd be a different, but reliable, smart watch.

I found that it could be restless alone or moving together in search for understanding.

Perhaps not reminiscent of a Norman Rockwell portrait, but often the image of me would be retreated from the bedroom, sitting on the couch, lamp on and Bible open, or any book for that matter. Late nights were ones with open minds. Anything for deeper meaning.

Stacking stones at the river as a means of soulful remembrance, a Buddhist perspective of Zen on the trail, what hiking with Nietzsche might be like. Stories of dreams, anecdotes about steps toward healing similar to what you are reading now, insights, perspectives, lived wisdom, lessons through suffering.

It didn't matter to me if the thoughts and ideas were Islamic, Christian, Buddhist, or Naturalists like Thoreau, Muir and Emerson, who held more complex religious beliefs but were drawn to God's creation for reasons all their own. I was open to it all. Any ideas that would resonate meaning.

It was on one of those nights that I came up with the idea to fashion a logo for *Heaven Hikes*, not for business, marketing, or promotion, but for something more personal. I wore a hat on most of my hikes and thought it would be meaningful to have one reserved only for *Heaven Hikes*, worn exclusively on the trail.

Another step in my pre-hike ritual, I imagined, a way of shifting my mind and body into that "special hiker named Jarrod." It would be a very private, very personal Clark Kent to Superman moment that I'm sharing here for the first time.

Drawing on some of my business savvy, I created the mark that would become the image on the hat. It is a line drawing of a hiker ascending a ridgeline, leading to a cross at the summit, radiating like a source of light, all enclosed within a cloud. The logo appeared in shades of blue on a patch, ironed onto an Old Legacy trucker hat. The mesh kept it cool, and the fit was snug and low-profile. Like George Whitefield with his personal seal, I too had found a symbolic way to express my pride and passion for *seeking heaven*.

TRUE BACKBONE

This next series of hikes would carry on that same spiritual renewal, in Spanish. In a word, each of the next four hikes, all above 10,000 feet, would begin with *San*, meaning Saint:

- San Antonio
- San Bernardino
- San Jacinto
- San Gorgonio

I was ready to hit the trail, my first mountain hike with a summit above 10,000 feet. The route stretched eleven miles, with about 4,000 feet of gain, and would take at least seven hours. My heart was open to let Mark Twain's wisdom ring true and to give this day a chance to be the most beautiful.

After parking near the Manker Flat trailhead, I followed my routine, cleared my head, geared up, whispered a silent prayer. An inward shout-out to my new motto, and I was off toward the summit of San Antonio, better known as Mt. Baldy, bound to *seek heaven* with every step.

This mountain serves more than a hiker's playground; it's also a skiing destination. That means there's always the temptation to cheat a little and take the lift up to where the real fun begins. I resisted, which meant walking three miles up a paved service road. It wasn't very scenic, but joined by other hikers, the energy of the day was starting to build. The burn in my legs and labored breathing, inevitable in the first couple miles of any big hike, arrived right on schedule.

The service road led to the Notch, a natural V-shaped clearing, a deep incision in the ridge carved over time by river flow and erosion. I had just come up one side along the canyon road. Now, from the other side, the world opened up. A panorama of cascading ridgelines, firs and pines, spilled into view. From this vantage point, the hike truly begins.

I had hit my stride now. With a fair number of long training hikes behind me, I even developed precision with my trekking poles. At times it felt almost as though I were gliding over scattered pine needles and rounding sharp switchbacks. Soon I reached one of the most striking features of Mt. Baldy, the ominous Devil's Backbone.

The spiny ridgeline stretches about a mile across a narrow path with sheer drops on either side. This was a "diamondback" moment for me. Like that thunderous snake encounter, I needed to focus, balance, and summon the presence of mind to traverse responsibly.

At one or two knife-edged bends, the Forest Service had bolted chains into the rock, intended as a self-assisted safeguard against unforgiving drops. Attentive and resolute, I made it safely across.

As I continued on, my mind turned to the paradox of crossing the Devil's Backbone in my own quest to seek heaven. Metaphorically speaking, of course, but it reminded me of the temptations and confusions I so often faced. That voice on my shoulder, whispering doubts about the worth of searching for closeness with God and Jarrod Jr in nature.

"That's absurd, Jarrod," the voice would say. "You're smart enough to know all you'll find in the wild are dead trees and animal scat." The whisper grew louder: "More death, nothing but crap." Persuasive, persistent, strong enough to wear me done, my fragile confidence eroding like the very cut in the mountain that carved the Notch.

Then came the final argument, sharp and tempting: "Call Fred. Grab a beer at that place you like. That's the six-pack that feels good. A cold one sounds a whole lot better than a hot day of painful steps on a path to nowhere." More than once, I'd given into that temptation. And it had led somewhere too, the all-too-personal sunrise blurred by sprinklers on a cemetery lawn.

As I trekked farther, my thoughts turned to Jesus' own encounter with temptation in the mountains. A Gospel account I'd heard many times over the years now spoke with new force. Matthew 4:1 sets the scene: *Then Jesus was led by the Spirit into the wilderness to be tempted by the devil.*

Fresh from the voice of Heaven declaring Him the Son of God, Jesus now faced the Devil's voice, weaving diabolical arts of persuasion, planting seeds of doubt. It was a test of faith, and each time Jesus met the lies with truth.

Reflecting on that story, I felt the weight of my own spiritual journey, the moments when I seemed carried in the arms of God, and the other times when the choices were mine alone to make. How fitting, I thought, that these reflections on good and evil would be born from a V-shaped valley, as though the mountain itself acknowledged the tension between the two.

As I reached the final push for the summit, there was a steep, rocky slope. It'd be about a mile from that point zig-zagging my way up, bracing myself with my poles and, at times, even using my hands. At about 10,000 feet of elevation, with the wind blowing, this proved to be the most challenging part of the hike. I made my way through it and stepped onto the summit, a flat plateau.

I sat down and took it all in. I made it to the top of peak number three, marking the halfway point in the *Six Pack*. The backbone itself could be seen in the distance, appearing smaller and less intimidating. Feeling physically, mentally and spiritually victorious, I glanced down with a nod of recognition. I had overcome the Devil's whisper and was now on top of San Antonio, enjoying a panoramic view of the San Gabrael and San Bernardino ranges, with San Jacinto and San Gorgonio off into the horizon.

I was surrounded by saints, and inspired to keep reaching, longer, farther and higher. There weren't any deep memories of Jarrod on this hike, but I felt closer to heaven for other reasons. My faith in this journey was strengthened.

That beer with Fred would have to wait. I still had miles of painful steps ahead, and I was certain they were leading me somewhere. Not entirely sure what that place would look like yet, but my imagination was beginning to form a vision. It would take a few more hikes, I told myself, before that picture sharpened into something I could truly see.

MORE LOVELINESS THAN LONELINESS

I decided to get an early start this time and arrived at the Angelus Oaks trailhead by 6 a.m. Today's hike to the summit of San Bernardino would be long and challenging. It would take more than nine hours, cover over fifteen miles, and climb nearly 4,700 feet. I quickly centered myself, readied my gear, and hit the trail, which began climbing right away.

This hike felt different from the very beginning. It was woodier, cooler, and shaded by black oak and cedar that offered welcome cover during the early switchbacks.

Manzanita thickets lined the trail, and I would come to see a lot of them on this climb. Their green foliage and smooth red bark became a usual companion, not only here but on the hikes to come. It was the season for them to be in bloom, showing clusters of delicate white and pink flowers. Later, their small red berries, *manzanita* being Spanish for "little apple," would appear.

I found myself fascinated by their resilience. Though wildfires consume mature manzanita plants, the seeds lying dormant in the soil, sometimes for decades, carry an armor-like shell. Fire can crack it open, triggering germination. Out of flames, new life emerges. Nature's resilience and renewal never cease to amaze.

The manzanitas brought to mind Matthew 3:11, when John the Baptist declares, *I baptize you with water for repentance. But after me comes one who is more powerful than I.... He will baptize you with the Holy Spirit and fire.*

What a living picture the manzanitas offered. In the wake of what would appear to be a wasteland, with loss stretching as far as the eye could see, a spark of renewal would begin to take shape. From the ashes, the phoenix would rise, reborn and triumphant. It offered an inspiring lens for my own quest in the wild.

As I continued climbing, I reached about the halfway point of the hike and came upon an unexpected discovery. A stone pile left behind by surveyors in the 1850s. Known as the Washington Monument, this cairn marked the origin point for maps and land division across Southern California. For me, it also marked the moment when memories of Jarrod began flooding back.

One in particular surfaced in vivid detail. Jennifer had often volunteered as a chaperone for Jarrod's class, but for one field trip she couldn't make it. That meant Dad was called off the bench. The outing was a full-day bus trip to San Diego for tide pool exploration.

I was excited to spend the day with Jarrod, though I was humbled the moment I walked into the classroom and the teacher greeted me with, "Oh, I've got you today." Clearly, he had been counting on a starting player for this one, and judging by his tone, I knew he thought he'd drawn the short straw. I silently agreed; he probably needed more than I was capable of. Still, we loaded onto the bus, and soon enough we were rolling southbound together.

There's something cool about being on a school bus with your son. It was as though I disappeared into the background, invisible to the chaos unfolding around me. Friends calling out to Jarrod. Girls giggled in his direction. Random things flew through the air. I probably should have been nforcing some kind of decorum, but readily enjoyed the anonymity.

True to his nature, Jarrod wasn't embarrassed to have me there, as some kids might have been. Maybe he was still too young for those insecurities. Either way, it was a fun, bumpy ride on that big yellow bus, complete with just the right amount of diesel exhaust to transport me instantly back to my own childhood rides.

When we shuffled off the bus and onto the beach, there was some initial organization, but soon enough the field trip seemed to come off the rails. What was supposed to be small groups of explorers quickly turned into the entire class scattering in every direction.

I was officially failing in my assigned role as chaperone, because Jarrod and I drifted off on our own. We poked at sea life floating in the pools, pointed things out, talked about whatever came to mind, but mostly we just enjoyed the sea breeze and the kind of comfortable silence that had always marked our time together.

Jarrod and I had an incredible way of getting lost in the moment. Whether it was playing catch at the park or acting out Star Wars battles at the foot of the stairs, it was almost as if we anticipated each other's moves, reading each other's minds. A laugh would often burst out before the words ever came.

This day at the beach was no different. We were locked in on one particular tide pool when we turned to see one of Jarrod's friends chasing another boy straight into the ocean, with the teacher frantically sprinting after them. Jarrod and I both laughed, and I realized once again my continuing failure as a chaperone.

Me & Jarrod Jr.
Laguna Beach Tide Pools
May, 2010 - 1st Grade

As unlucky as that teacher was to end up with me, I was beyond lucky to have been given that day with Jarrod. I think back on it often, especially when I hear Terry Jack's *Seasons in the Sun.* The words feel as though they were written into the sand for us that very day:

> *We had joy, we had fun, we had seasons in the sun. But the stars we could reach were just starfish on the beach.*

The switchbacks stretched into longer runs through dense forest. I passed Jeffrey pine with scattered manzanitas along the way, when suddenly bursts of color appeared. One meadow seemed to radiate wild bouquets, purple lupine, yellow columbine, and the fiery reds and oranges of Indian paintbrush. Not long after this vibrant stretch, the trail crested onto the summit. A wide clearing dotted with granite boulders and wind-bent limber pines barely holding on.

The views were panoramic. A reminder of why those early surveyors chose this place as such an important set of coordinates. From here, the whole of Southern California, mountains, deserts, and sprawling suburbs, came into complete focus. I had reached peak number four.

These mountains were proving to be a powerful world for me. Back at that colorful meadow there was no one in sight, and the peak itself was mine alone, a private encounter.

Edward Abbey, affectionately known as "Cactus Ed," once wrote in *Desert Solitaire* that being twenty miles from the nearest human felt more like loveliness than loneliness, even a quiet exultation.

I felt that truth here. The higher I climbed, the farther I moved from the world below, the closer it seemed I was edging toward Heaven.

This mindset was about to be challenged with the next hike. My aim was already fixed on the next summit, rugged, and one of the most spectacular hikes anywhere.

San Jacinto, here I come.

A WINK AND A PRAYER

I had decided to hike around Idyllwild, to prep for San Jacinto. One of the approaches to the peak is reachable from this area but mine would be a less strenuous choice. The plan this time was to spend a weekend at a B&B in this charming mountain town that has long attracted artists, writers and musicians. I was sold on the idea when learning the mayor was a golden retriever named Max.

As I settled into my room, I was immediately taken in by this oasis of a mountain community. Approachable a few different ways, whichever road taken seems to come upon the village that is the center of town. An abrupt but warm welcome with all its storefronts that come into view.

There was a silent auction at the B&B, with a wine reception to attract bidders. The cause was local and the donated items also seemed to be local, arts and crafts, exactly the kinds of creative handywork you'd expect from Max's friends. I bid on a surprise item that I'd find out later was a very odd kaleidoscope.

As the sun set, what really appeared to be Idyllwild's well-kept secret was the night sky. Looking up, I was reminded of the true distance the heavens really are, but at the same time, the awe of how close those stars appear in the moonlight. Although I had agreed with Cactus Ed earlier, something I hadn't felt in a long time, came over me. This moment would be better spent with someone else. Maybe it was time to consider "loveliness" with my fellow humans.

It was a weekend of hiking in Idyllwild that proved both rewarding and humbling. One hike in particular hurt more than it should have. I misjudged the distance, pushed farther than I planned, and ran out of water on the way back. By the time I reached the trailhead and collapsed at my car, I downed a full liter of water and needed twenty minutes just to collect myself before driving back to the hotel.

Lesson learned, hikes should be planned and understood ahead of time, not taken casually, and bringing extra water is definitely a smart move. My prep had been solid, but I walked away with more. Was it a manzanita seed moment? I wasn't sure, but a few days later, what grew from that experience was the courage to create a *Christian Mingle* profile.

Another couple of weeks passed before I laced up again. That spacing had become my routine, time for recovery, reflection, and a reset, so I'd be ready to absorb the full weight of the next climb.

Unlike Baldy, the San Jacinto adventure began not with a service road but with a ride, very much warranted this time. The Palm Springs Aerial Tramway carries you swiftly from the desert floor to 8,500 feet, depositing you in a clearing that immediately immerses you in mountain wilderness.

For the first steps, though, in full hiking regalia, you share the path with kids clutching ice cream cones from the tramway shop. Soon enough, the cones vanish, the crowd thins, and the hike becomes very real. The thought of ice cream drifts to the back of your mind, waiting there as the prize envisioned for the return.

Although Palm Springs is famously known for its unrelenting desert heat in summer, at this elevation the day was cooler, shaded by lush forests. The trail through Long Valley followed a creek, a scenic and gentle stretch of the hike. It carried a truly authentic alpine feel, softer and more welcoming than the stark climbs of Baldy or the endless grind of San Bernardino. I loved those hikes, but Jacinto was different.

As it turned out, the grind would come soon enough. The sights and sounds of the creek gave way to switchbacks carved into the mountain, where steeper steps led over loose rock and uneven footing. My trekking poles, long past any chance of being returned to REI, now carried the scars of the journey, dings and scrapes that testified to my progress on the Six-Pack Challenge.

At this point I was almost a passenger, trusting the muscle memory and instincts I had developed. Just as I had become a glider over pine needles on Baldy, here I was traversing rocks and gaps without thinking, letting the tempo carry me forward.

About five miles in, I reached Wellman Divide, the natural lunch stop. I sat on a boulder and enjoyed a gourmet trail feast of beef jerky, granola, and apple slices. From this spot, craggy ridges stretched into the distance as far as the eye could see. As comfortable as the stop was, I quickly learned that too much downtime meant stiff legs and burning muscles. So, with trusty poles in hand, I pushed on.

Soon the dense forest thinned into rugged outcroppings, the ground rough with rock, and the seasoned shapes of lodgepoles and limber pines appeared. The limbers were an especially welcome sight, not only a sign of higher progress but also a beauty in themselves, with bluish-green needles and long, heavy cones.

By now, I had come to greet these trees as old friends, picking up their soft, bendable needles, crushing them in my hands, and tossing them into the air for a breath of pine, sharp and resinous, with hints of vanilla, and the pleasure of feeling their texture.

This time, curious, I took it a step farther. One needle stuck to my fingers, and I chewed it. The taste was bitter, but it was something new, another way to interact with the mountain. I realized I was becoming closer, more curious, drawn deeper into nature with every step.

As I trekked along, my thoughts wandered back to the profile I had put up on the website. Feeling insecure about the whole idea, I was second-guessing myself. To my surprise, my inbox was filling up quickly, and I wasn't sure what to make of it. Do I respond to everyone? What exactly does a "wink" mean? And a card…was that like a wink and a nod? It was humbling, in its own way, to be "liked," even if it came only as an alert lighting up my screen. But was I ready to "like" back?

Ironically, my thoughts turned to a memory of Jarrod, who became a source of regained confidence. Jillian often hosted sleepovers, four or five of her closest school friends filling the house with laughter. Most of the fun stayed in her room, but sometimes it spilled into the game room upstairs, next to the kids' bedrooms. Jarrod's room was right next door.

As modest and reserved as he usually was, Jarrod saw these nights as his chance to put on a show. He'd stride out shirtless, playing it off as if he hadn't noticed the room full of girls. It was, of course, the perfect time to shoot hoops with the Nerf basket hanging from his now-wide-open door, perfectly framed for an audience.

The response was always the same. Jillian rolling her eyes in disgust, her friends whispering just loud enough for him to hear, "Oh, your brother is so cute." I smiled at the memory. Maybe I could borrow a little of that bravado later. Maybe I'd even learn how to "wink," I thought.

The switchbacks climbed higher until the trail opened into a clearing where a stone shelter seemed to melt into the mountain itself. From there, the only way was up, a scramble across massive granite boulders to the craggy crown of San Jacinto. This summit was no flat plateau or gentle crest. It was a rugged fortress of slabs and stone, the mountain declaring itself with raw grandeur.

A few of us hikers shared the peak, but at nearly 11,000 feet, the second-highest point in Southern California, it still felt like solitude. I stretched out on one of those long slabs of granite, hands behind my head, legs crossed, a lounge chair in the clouds. Heaven was within reach, I thought, at least the parts of it that could be grasped.

The whistle of the wind bouncing off the rocks, the chill in the air, made that granite lounge-chair feel more coastal than mountaintop. Five down, one to go. This Six-Pack had become something far more consequential than I expected.

I imagined that Steller's Jay back at Wilson might chatter in recognition. Perhaps I had even earned the respect of the rattler at Cucamonga. These peaks were becoming chapters in a storybook, bound together with the tales of countless other hikers, each of us climbing for our own reasons.

As Thoreau wrote in *Walden*, during his own quest for self-discovery in nature, "Heaven is under our feet as well as over our heads." I was beginning to believe it. These hikes were less about spacecraft and more about mindset. Heaven was here on earth, as much as in any distant world. Maybe I should have paid closer attention to Belinda Carlisle, who belted back in the '80s, "Heaven is a place on earth."

It was becoming clear that heaven wasn't something to be chased, but something revealed through openness and movement. With each step, it felt less distant and more intimate, something I could touch, carry, and return to. Being fully present where I stood, faithful to the moment and what it offered, was enough. The more I slowed down and paid attention, the clearer it became that what I was searching for wasn't above or beyond me, but unfolding right where my feet met the ground.

One more summit remained, Old Grayback, San Gorgonio, the highest point in Southern California at over 11,500 feet. For a more intimate San Jacinto summit picture, I placed two paracord bracelets on the slab where I had rested. I had designed them, and a friend made them for me, military-grade, with a heart at the center, born from another late-night creative escapade. One for me, one for Jarrod. It felt right. This hike had stirred something inside a wounded heart. Was there love in the air? I wasn't sure. But the idea, and the possibility, was beginning to take shape.

SHUFFLING INTO SUNRISE

It would be nearly a month before I made my push for the last of the Six Peaks. Business travel and a busier-than-usual schedule kept me grounded, though I stayed fresh with shorter hikes and time on the bike. Gorgonio was always in view, the prize ahead.

In the meantime, I responded to a few messages in my inbox. I wasn't bold enough to initiate a like or a wink, but I worked up the nerve to wink back a couple of times. Most of it amounted to little more than pen-pal exchanges. One of the benefits of this modern approach, I realized, was the safe distance it provided. Nothing really clicked. At least not until it did.

A "hello" card came through just as I happened to be online, which wasn't often. Truthfully, I was drifting away from the whole thing, retreating into the comfort of solitude, even off the trails. My thoughts leaned more toward buying a cabin in Idyllwild and entrusting my heart to the wilderness, and Max, than chasing the dating scene. Those thoughts were speaking louder than the prospect of meeting someone new. This card, though, tugged me back, pulling me from the brink of my own Walden experiment.

When I opened the card and traced it back to its sender, her picture, her profile, I was spellbound. The feeling was immediate and impossible to put fully into words. She was stunningly beautiful, yes, but it was more than that. In her story, I saw hints of vulnerability and sensitivity that resonated with my own cautious attempts at transparency.

I responded, and we began to exchange emails. The standard volley of introductions, covering work, interests, church life, favorite foods. Subtle but intentional questions slipped in as safeguards, meant to uncover red flags that might hint at "stranger danger."

One question was about favorite bands. I answered with Depeche Mode, New Order, and The Cure. Her reply came quickly, just six words:

"I think we can be friends."

Her name was Erin. She lived nearly 200 miles away, on the Central Coast. But distance didn't matter. We began writing often, and in the weeks that followed, her messages became the brightest part of my days.

The time had come to finish the challenge. It wasn't the Seven Summits of the world, but as the highest of the *Six Pack* of Peaks, San Gorgonio was my Everest. The day ahead promised at least ten hours, eighteen miles, and some 5,400 feet of gain to reach the summit.

I parked at Forest Falls and stepped onto the Vivian Creek Trailhead at 5 a.m., beginning with a crossing of the dry wash of the Mill Creek riverbed. On the far side of the gray stones lay the gateway into the forest, which enveloped me almost immediately. This was no gentle start like San Jacinto, here the mountain revealed itself right away, a staircase pitched steeply up the slope.

Just as the burn set in, a fire in my legs hotter than usual, I had a surprising and welcome encounter. A mule deer, close enough that we startled each other.

Beautiful creatures, with their tawny coats and big, swiveling ears. For a moment we both stood still, curious rather than wary. That's the gift of being on the trail at dawn, I thought; by the time the crowds arrived, the deer would be long gone. We exchanged a look that seemed to last, then gracefully parted ways, one of us moving far faster than the other.

After a brutal start, I reached Vivian Creek Camp, where the sound of running water mixed with the resounding click of my poles, and for a short stretch, the trail eased. Not for long, though. Over the next few miles, the path wound deeper into the wilderness, the forest thickening, the sense of remoteness growing, all while the ascent pressed on.

The push was constant and demanding. A few times I had to pause, leaning on my poles to catch my breath, before moving again. Finally, at about four miles in, I arrived at Halfway Camp, resting just over 8,000 feet. The summit was nowhere in sight. If anything, that invisible crown made it clear that the rest of the hike would be the true test.

The trail climbed higher, brushing me against the company of my favorite limber pines before leading into the long switchbacks that delivered me to High Creek Camp, around 9,200 feet. Here I allowed myself a break and a bite. A Clif Bar and some trail mix, fuel for the miles still ahead. Lunch would wait for the broad, flat bench of Gorgonio's summit, I'd planned.

As I sat, legs grateful for even a brief rest, I noticed the cadence of the day had pulled me into step with a few other hikers. Some labored behind, some pressed just ahead, but for miles now we had become a loose group without names or conversation. A nod, a grin, a shared wince was enough to bind us.

Each of us had chosen to wake at dawn on a Saturday morning, leaving warm beds for the voluntary hardship of steep trails and burning lungs. The tradeoff was the same for us all. Clean air, expansive views, and the chance to feed whatever inner hunger had drawn us here.

The poet Rumi captured it better than I ever could:

The breezes at dawn have secrets to tell you.
Don't go back to sleep.
You must ask for what you want.
Don't go back to sleep.

Refueled and ready, I was back on the trail. Ahead, countless switchbacks climbed the mountain's shoulder as far as I could see. A couple of those familiar hikers who hadn't stopped when I did were now dots in the distance, our separate stories still weaving together. I found my stride again, the poles setting the tone, my mind drifting. As I shuffled along, a memory of Jarrod shuffled in.

This one was from a school dance, another one of my very rare stints as a chaperone, maybe the only other time. It turned into a precious glimpse of Jarrod in a special setting. At the time, one of his favorite bands was LMFAO, the duo famous for *Party Rock Anthem* and its repeated lyric: *Every day I'm shufflin'*. The song came with its own dance move, not unlike the "running man" of my youth, except this version seemed to cover twice as much ground. And Jarrod took it to another level entirely.

Classic Jarrod, low-key until he wasn't. The dance floor was just starting to stir, a small group testing the waters. Then the DJ dropped *Party Rock Anthem*, and Jarrod sprang into action. Not a wallflower that day. He practically ice-skated across the gym floor, shuffling with precision, gliding in and out of traffic. Within seconds, two, then three other boys fell in behind him as though a magnetic force had been released. Soon the cluster of kids that had been the center of attention just moments earlier had formed around them. Jarrod suddenly, unmistakably, at the lead.

I remember standing with a teacher, both of us smiling, watching the whole thing unfold. I said something like, "Full of surprises, isn't he?" After the song ended, Jarrod slipped easily back into the crowd, danced a little longer, then wandered over to chat with a couple of friends who hadn't left the sidelines.

It was such a gift, that ability he had to turn it on and off at will, to go from zero to sixty in five seconds flat, then just as quickly coast back to idle. He could be the life of the party if he chose, or the attentive friend alongside someone outside the action.

I was at 10,500 feet now. The tree line was fading, the path underfoot more broken rock and sand than pine needles, the air noticeably thinner. Gusty winds swept across the ridge as the views opened wide. A clear sightline to San Jacinto, my last peak, now appearing almost eye level. After what felt like endless switchbacks, I stepped onto the ridge and finally saw the summit itself. From there it was a firm push, another 500 feet, until the trail delivered me onto the broad, rocky plateau of San Gorgonio Peak.

I had made it to *Old Grayback*, above the trees, standing in the clouds. From this vantage, the ranges spread in every direction. To the south, San Jacinto; to the west, Baldy; together they framed me in a perfect triangle. I lifted the summit sign high, and another hiker kindly snapped the photo. The Six-Pack of Peaks challenge was complete. Standing there, I could look back across the many miles and mountains that had brought me to this place.

In just a few months I had found purpose, and with it, a way not only to keep moving but to arrive at a destination. The perspective I held at the start, or what I had thought of as my odyssey, had shifted along the way.

I had been convinced that heaven was distant, and that Jarrod was equally distant from me. What I discovered in the wilderness, felt deep in my heart, was that heaven was closer than I imagined.

I could feel Jarrod, see him, remember him, share my life with him. We were still together. I had walked into the wisdom T. S. Eliot spoke of:

The end of all our exploring will be to arrive where we started and know the place for the first time.

These peaks would not be my last. Nature had become my heaven on earth, the place where my mind grew still and where I felt closest to Jarrod. The *Heaven Hikes* would continue. The trials and trails of my odyssey were not over. I longed to draw nearer to God, His creation, His angel. But there was something else stirring, too.

A new sunrise was breaking. I could feel its warmth on my face. It was real, and I wanted to see where this new day would lead. *See, I am doing a new thing! Now it springs up; do you not perceive it? I am making a way in the wilderness and streams in the wasteland* (Isaiah 43:19).

Perhaps Act Two was waiting, where my wounded heart might open again, to the kind of loveliness found not only in mountains, but in others.

Blessings were on the horizon, more than I could have imagined.

PART III
New Dawn

7
FAB FIVE, BLENDED & UNBREAKABLE

And over all these virtues put on love, which binds them all together in perfect unity.

—Colossians 3:14

There's no person in the whole world like you, and I like you just the way you are.

—Fred Rogers

The family is one of nature's masterpieces.

—George Santayana
(The Life of Reason)

Erin and I had met a few times, taking things slow but enjoying each other's company. We'd already done the obligatory family meet-and-greet, with chaperones present, to confirm all was off to a safe start.

Then came an unforgettable night at the Santa Barbara Bowl, where we saw New Order in concert. We'd even had a night at the Cherry Festival playing carnival games, like a couple of high school kids on a Friday night.

For our next outing, we planned something more active. Erin would come to my place near Palm Springs, and we'd ride a canyon bike trail, about twenty-five miles round trip. Erin wasn't a regular cyclist, but she loved the outdoors and was up for the adventure. I had a spare bike ready. It would be our first time really playing outside, beyond the usual dinners, concerts, and movie dates.

Erin had this game she liked to play, and it quickly became a fun way for us to get to know each other. It was called *Five Questions*. We'd take turns asking each other a series of questions, with the understanding that nothing was really off-limits. Sometimes the questions were light and playful, other times deeper, but always drawing us closer. One of my early answers leaned into how much I love cycling, so this planned outing was Erin being both a good listener and a good sport.

The ride started off like a dream, perfect weather, not too hot. For the first few miles we coasted side by side, talking easily. We even touched on how we might introduce our kids someday, my Jillian, her Kaitlyn, and her six-year-old son, Andrew. At that time Kaitlyn was about the same age Jarrod Jr. would have been, and Jillian was just a few years older.

The San Timoteo Canyon Road wound its way toward Redlands, with a couple of scenic stops along the way, including an old schoolhouse dating back to the 1880s. We cruised along and took breaks here and there. But on the way back, I realized my idea of fun was probably unfair. As much of a good sport as Erin was, we only made it halfway before she hit the proverbial wall.

At a place called Fisherman's Retreat, she surrendered to a patch of grass, completely spent. I felt awful about pushing her so far, and didn't want to leave her there long. My next mission was clear. Get back to the house as fast as possible, grab the car, and return with water. I must have looked like I was in an Olympic time trial, pedaling as fast as I could, until I rolled back up, car, cold water, and rescue in hand.

Erin assured me all was fine; she had just underestimated her own limits. Feeling like a rookie, I realized I needed to be more careful. Still, what emerged was a clear next step: broadening our plans to include those closest to us, starting with the kids.

We were about to embark on a completely new kind of journey, one of filling hearts with new love. There were bound to be storms ahead as the magic formed, but we'd both pray for help, trusting that *"God sets the lonely in families...."* (Psalm 68:6).

OUTSTRETCHED HANDS

Over the next few months, we planned plenty of family time. The kids clicked right away, more easily than we could have hoped. Jillian and Andrew especially. Their bond seemed effortless, with no influence on our part beyond bringing them together. The rest took care of itself. Jillian's big-sister energy found Andew easily, while his gentle, playful nature reached someplace tender in her wounded heart.

One evening on Stern's Wharf in Santa Barbara captured it fully. There was a chill in the air, and I gave Jillian my sweater. As we looked out over the ocean horizon, awaiting the sunset, our attention shifted to something even more beautiful. Jillian and Andrew were zipped together inside that oversized sweater, his head peeking out, both of them smiling, a reminder that the heart knows things the mind cannot explain.

Another unforgettable moment came on a road trip to Mesa Verde National Park. We decided to stop at the Grand Canyon. A break from the car time, and what better change of scenery than one of the World's natural wonders. We'd make the best of the few hours we had, which led us to hop aboard a shuttle tour. The final stop was a breathtaking lookout, set on a plateau adjacent to a visitor center.

The kids were taking in the canyon view when the weather shifted. Light rain at first, then suddenly a gusty downpour. As if sensing real danger, they moved in close, arms around each other tight. The group hug lasted only a minute or two before we all headed inside the visitor center to comfortably wait it out. Feeling like reaching a destination more than making a detour, it was our first glimpse of how Jillian, Kaitlyn and Andrew had bonded and begun to look out for one another.

As momentum was building between the kids, Erin and I planned another trip, this time to Joshua Tree, for a more hands-on opportunity to win over that same enthusiasm the kids were showing toward each other, this time among the adults.

Joshua Tree turned out be the perfect landscape to lose ourselves in the moment and let our guards down. Like a natural playground, we climbed boulders, wandered desert trails, and made our way to lookout points that were less storm and more fun than at the Grand Canyon.

The Joshua Tree itself was named by Mormon pioneers who saw its outstretched arms as the biblical Joshua, guiding them to the promised land. To me, it was another of nature's monuments to strength within God's creation, showing how to stand tall in the harshest conditions, striking that perfect balance between beauty and resilience.

In its quirky trees and sculpted rocks, Joshua Tree carried the same *Heaven-Hikes* energy, a place where strength and beauty lived side by side, inviting us to trust, open our hearts, and continue on our path to build something new together.

There were sparks from Joshua Tree that carried on in the months that followed. We had even fashioned a name for our new group, the *Fab Five*. Andrew and I began spending time together, just the two of us, outings between the beaches of the Central Coast and desert, a manageable distance, and one that gave us an exciting variety.

It wasn't lost on me that I was falling in love with someone who had a son near the same age Jarrod was when he was called to heaven. On the surface it might seem like mere coincidence, but in my heart, it felt like a blessing. I knew how lucky I was to have the chance to be Andrew's friend, to offer some gentle dad energy.

I wasn't sure yet what role I might ultimately play, but I cherished the friendship that was forming. *Every good and perfect gift is from above, coming down from the Father of the heavenly lights, who does not change like shifting shadows* (James 1:17).

REAL AND IMAGINED

Beyond the adventures in nature, I met Andrew where he was. His talents and sense of adventure seemed limitless, his energy off the charts, day and night. He introduced me to disc golf and airsoft. We shot hoops, tossed the football, and spent hours chasing Charizard, Pikachu, and other, Pokémon all across town. It actually became a shared obsession, best summed up in a single event.

One evening, while driving to the Goleta Pier, a hunter's paradise for Pokémon, a rare find popped up on Andrew's phone. They don't stick around long, which meant stopping the car fast, right inside the parking lot but far from any real space. We jumped out and dashed into the bushes. Caught up in the moment, I completely missed the sheriff's cruiser parked nearby. To him, it must have looked like a man and a boy had just abandoned their car and disappeared into the dark, probable cause for investigation if there ever was one.

Andrew and I scored the prize quickly, then walked back to find a uniformed officer standing by our car, flashlight pointed our way. Somehow, in a mix of excitement and that caught-in-the-act feeling, I explained the name of the Pokémon we'd gone after and how rare it was to find in the wild. All I can say is the officer must have been a dad himself, because he smiled and simply advised me to park the car properly if we decided to chase down any more.

TRAILING BESIDE KAITLYN

Early that next summer, Kaitlyn and I had an adventure all our own, one that even left her adventurous brother in the dust. We joined Erin's family for a church camp in South Tahoe, and together the whole group set out for a hike on Mt. Tallac. The goal wasn't to reach the peak, which rises just shy of 10,000 feet. Tallac is a strenuous ten-mile trek, taking about seven hours with nearly 3,500 feet of vertical gain. At the summit lies a prize worth the effort, a sweeping view of Big Blue and the jewel of Emerald Bay.

The family began with the short lakefront trail near the base of the mountain, about a half-mile stroll through meadows, wetlands, and forest floor, with Tallac towering above and Floating Island Lake gleaming across the way.

As the trail steepened into switchbacks, people slowly peeled off. About a mile in, most turned back toward camp. Three of us pressed on, Kaitlyn, her cousin Courtney, and me. Courtney was an experienced hiker. Kaitlyn was taking on her first mountain hike. In the context of the *Six Pack* of Peaks I'd completed a few months earlier, Tallac was comparable to Mt. Baldy. She was starting three levels higher than I had when my challenge began.

Finishing was still not the goal, more like, let's see how far we can go and enjoy the views along the way. I was excited to have time with Kaitlyn. She is an extraordinarily talented singer and musical theater performer, accomplished both inside and outside of school, even sharing stages with well-known musicians for local events. I'd been captivated by her performances, but we hadn't yet shared an adventure of our own. Sometimes those moments, carved out on a trail, turn into the best kind of bonding.

Mt. Tallac was special in its own right. A large snowfield lingers on its east face well into summer, visible from the lake and trailhead below. Over the years, it has cut across the mountain in such a way that it forms a striking white cross. Early settlers, as far back as the 1800s, knew Tallac as "the mountain with the cross."

On this *Heaven Hike*, it felt less like coincidence and more like a written invitation. The stage was set for Kaitlyn and me, a duet in nature. I'd try and measure up.

With Big Blue at our backs, we began the ascent into the wooded trail. We passed alongside lakes, where the grind began to intensify. I was without my trusty poles this time. It was an unassisted walk in the wilderness. Higher up, the trail alternated between shaded forest and open, rocky stretches. At each bend, Kaitlyn accepted encouragement from both her cousin and me to keep going. We had crossed the point of no return. The prize ahead was worth pressing on, knowing that the breathtaking view would have to be earned.

I was proud of Kaitlyn in that moment. She dug deep, channeling her inner strength, buoyed by her cousin's gentle nudges and my approving nods, which fueled her steps. At last, the summit ridge came into view. From there it was a light scramble across rocky talus, leading to the summit itself. The summit presented like an open palm of stone, as if the mountain were lifting a hand to reveal a view it was all too proud to share. A panorama unfolded before us of one of the most beautiful alpine lakes in the world.

Kaitlyn was visibly exhausted. The thin air, paired with the steady push the mountain demanded, was beginning to show itself. She'd find her stride again on the way down, but I smiled and offered a warm-hearted congratulations, knowing how much effort it had taken.

This hike remains a fond memory, one that sparked our bond. We had found a favorite song together, one written in nature, and in our hearts.

ANDREW'S RAINBOW

Lake Tahoe is a nature lover's paradise, and we weren't finished by a long shot. The next day, Andrew and I had an early rise. His adventure was only a sunrise away. This time, it wasn't a mountaintop we were after. Trout was on our minds. Fly rods would be in our hands, with a local guide, nicknamed "the bug guy," to show us around the Truckee River.

Meanwhile, my legs were sore, and truthfully, a relaxing campfire sounded like the perfect finale for a day to remember. As part of our pull-together, the *Fab Five* had invested in a mid-size travel trailer. Branded "Mighty Lite" by the factory, the name stuck. That night, it gave us one of the best sleeps ever.

It was still dark when we loaded into the truck and got on our way, for what would be a short drive to the stretch of the Truckee our guide promised was a well-kept secret and bountiful river run.

We pulled in and parked. The bug guy was already crouched near the water, lifting rocks and pulling jars from his backpack, a literal Petri dish of nymphs that had just hatched, guiding us to the best bait to lead our lines in the water. I'd learned long ago why it's called fishing, not catching; there are no guarantees. But with a guide and fresh bugs, the odds were better.

In my mind, though, it was all about Andrew. His first time on the river. Never handled a fly rod, never touched a trout. I hoped his rainbow was coming. Maybe the whole experience would catch, something Andrew and I could share all our own. One day, maybe, even casting into that famous line from A *River Runs Through It*.

"In our family, there's no clear line between religion and fly fishing."

For now, I was determined to get him a fish. But the "clear line" our guide and I kept setting for Andrew quickly turned into a tangled mess before it hit the water. It was obvious we needed more prep. I'd seen Andrew flick his wrist in a forehand throw on the disc golf course, sending a frisbee gliding into chains that turned heads, mine included. He had the skill, the touch, and the focus.

This would be on-the-job training in fly fishing mechanics. A forward cast at ten o'clock, a back cast at two. The tricky part was the pause in between, timing that flick so the line stayed straight, the hook coming to rest just right. Not easy, but like a disc golf throw, everyone's cast develops its own signature. And Andrew was already leaning in with the concentration to claim his own style.

With some practice, and a few tangles wrestled out of the line, Andrew began to channel his young Brad Pitt. The only thing missing was the narrow-brim cowboy hat. His cast fell into place like a brilliant musical composition, the line zigzagging through the air in a pattern I was sure would charm any hungry trout. Still, no fish.

Then, as if by magic, the beauty of fishing revealed itself. The gift came as a surprise. *"Fish on!"* The call rang from the sidelines, a reminder for Andrew to firmly pull and set the hook. In that instant, the bug guy and I became wing-men, him in the water with the net, me an arm's length away, ready to assist. Andrew held secure. His rainbow trout flashed into view. Bug scooped, and suddenly, it was show-time. Andrew had caught his first fish.

I thought of Jarrod in that moment. We had many adventures together, but we never went fishing. Seeing Andrew's joy, holding the trout proudly with both hands extended, just far enough to make it look a little bigger, I felt Jarrod's approval wash over me, as if he were standing there with us.

Over time, I would often think how quickly Andrew and Jarrod would have become friends. Both kind-natured, both adventurous without limits. Andrew, like his sister, loved the stage, more center spotlight than Jarrod, but I know they would have found the light together.

Soon, I would be introduced to Andrew's habit of breaking randomly into the "floss" dance, the one with arms swinging back and forth. I could picture him and Jarrod side by side, one flossing, the other shuffling, both laughing, together, alive in the moment and lost in imagination.

LAKE REFLECTIONS

Tahoe wasn't finished with us yet, or maybe it was my turn, to claim a little of that loveliness in solitude. The past few days had been amazing, inspiring even, stirring me to find my Zen in the wild, to soak it all in and think.

Our *Fab Five* was gelling. I had to silence that whisper from the Devil's Backbone, the one still trying to tell me that the Walden dream of Idyllwild was my destiny. At least by now, it had given up on convincing me to have that beer with Fred.

There were several more hikes in Tahoe that left an impression. Mt. Tallac remained the most beautiful in my opinion. Freel Peak, the highest in that stretch of the Sierra Nevada at over 10,800 feet, stood as tall as San Jacinto, one of my beloved *Six Pack*. Heavenly, world-renowned as a ski resort in winter, offered an equally spectacular summit in the summer, rising to more than 10,000 feet. I would eventually bag these peaks during a future church camp trip.

This time, though, the biker shorts won the coin toss. It wouldn't be the organized century ride that takes place each year around Big Blue, but I had my sights on the same respectable challenge. Tomorrow, I'd ride my bike the 72 miles all the way around the lake. Known as *America's Most Beautiful Bike Ride,* it promised more than 4,000 feet of calf-burning climbs, clicking into low gears, up off the saddle, grinding up the grades. Brutal, yes, but as the name promised, the pain would be worth the gain.

It would only be me waking up at the crack of dawn. I was missing church camp today but would be in worship and awe of God's creation, inviting the smell of pine, breathing in fresh mountain air, feeling the warm embrace of the sun, mixed with alpine coolness. *Holy, holy, holy is the Lord Almighty; the whole earth is full of his glory* (Isaiah 6:3).

Coming out of the campground, the logical direction to take is clockwise, up the California side, then around the lake back down the Nevada side, waving at the casinos on the way to the finish. The one thing hiking and biking has in common is that ticket for admission, the burn the legs feel during the first couple miles, warming up the engine.

The motor was revving good for the first several miles to the first attraction, a look out over Emerald Bay. I wouldn't take an endless reel, but at some milestones like this one, it was a Kodak moment, selfie to show Erin later. Maybe it was the determined look on my face or how the picture framed but me with my bike caught the attention of a photojournalist for a travel mag, so the claim was, and the request to take my picture. Why not, if anything, subtle acknowledgement that I at least looked the part.

I kept a fixed cadence, pausing now and then for a breath, a sip of water, or simply to take in the more wooded stretches where I was utterly alone in the wilderness. These stretches held that "loneliness and loveliness" blend, the very recipe that seemed to open my mind. With only the sound of tires rolling over the road, I had the presence to reflect on all that had transpired.

It had been more than a year now. Erin and I had grown very close, and I was deeply in love. Even admitting that to myself still felt startling. Never, not even in my clearest moments of reflection, on or off the trail, had I thought such a reality was possible again.

Like Theodore Roosevelt, I had resolved to keep moving, but for so long it had felt as though the light had gone out in my life.

Yet now, somehow, a fire burned within me. I almost felt like a child again, dreaming, longing, and still more spellbound than that first night I had received Erin's card.

That part of my heart, I once believed, was as hollow as those ghostly trees on Cucamonga's peak, still standing, yes, clinging on, but with the vibrant life of their prime long gone. Only memory remained, a haunting shadow of what was. And yet, against all odds, something new had taken root.

Unable to explain it, I found myself thinking about the future, what it might be like to be married again, to have a family, to be whatever Andrew and Kaitlyn would allow me to be.

I knew titles and roles mattered less than presence in their lives. Even that whisper of dissent that would normally crush my fragile spirit was met with the same absolute truth

Jesus used to silence the lies thrown at Him. *The Lord is my strength and my shield; my heart trusts in him, and he helps me. My heart leaps for joy, and with my song I praise him* (Psalm 28:7).

By now I was about 27 miles into the ride. The sun wasn't harsh, but the climbs had already added to the workout. Approaching the Tahoe City Dam, I spotted an ice cream shop, the Tahoe Creamery, and decided it was the perfect place to stop. Inside, I found others in the same characteristic uniform of clip-in cycling shoes clinking on the floor, tight shorts, zip-up jerseys.

One rider asked where I was headed. "All the way around," I said. He smirked and replied, "Well, that's the goal anyway."

Maybe it was the brain freeze from the ice cream, but his words stuck with me. Interesting, I thought. Yes, it was the goal, but I hadn't questioned it, or even considered the possibility of less. He'd never know it, but I appreciated that reminder. It confirmed for me that my confidence was solid, my gaze sure across the handlebars, my course set.

I was not just chasing a goal; I was on an odyssey. I kept moving with the words of Gene Kranz echoing in my mind: *failure is not an option.*

The next milestone in the ride was Zephyr Cove. All the climbing up to Spooner Summit, the hardest part, was finally behind me. Pointed downhill now, I launched into the effortless flight of descending several hundred feet. It felt like being strapped to the rocket ship Gene Kranz had sling-shotted around the moon, and in my head, I was screaming... *"goooooals!"* A silent nod to Jarrod on his kick-scooter, while I held on tight.

Then the pedals came back into play. I settled into a moderate cadence across the state line and onto the Nevada side. The North Shore carried me past casino-lined roads, less scenic than the alpine stretches but still leading me forward toward that oasis of wild beauty where I'd started.

By the time Mighty Lite came into view, it was about 4 p.m., eleven hours after I had clipped in at 5 a.m., with plenty of stops along the way.

The trailer was empty; everyone else was still at Bible studies, outings, or enjoying the church chuckwagon setup for an early dinner. Inside, the A/C felt like an icebox. My thought was just to lie down for a few minutes before catching up with the gang. That "few minutes" stretched into a few hours. What a great day. What a great trip, I thought.

That picture I'd barely begun to imagine earlier was now showing its outlines more clearly. Maybe the scene would be more Rockwell-inspired than I had first believed, ordinary moments, shaded with meaning, framed in love.

BEAUTIFULLY SHAPED

Not all of the building blocks came from long car rides or special attractions. Some came right at home. T.S. Eliot's words returned to me, just as true now as when I first discovered heaven underfoot, reminding me again that I had arrived back where I started, with a renewed perspective and heart. This time, it was Jarrod's room, and those piles of Legos. Unfinished business.

What it felt like then was a puzzle I could never solve. I didn't have all the pieces. Jarrod's imagination, his hands, those were not mine, as much as I wanted them to be. That pile of Legos had always paralyzed me in grief, drawing me back into the same place of darkness.

Now, though, this was a new sunrise, with an awakened heart. I felt Jarrod with me, not pressing me to finish what he started, but inviting me to build new things together. The Lord's words in Ezekiel 36:26 gave me truth: *I will give you a new heart and put a new spirit in you; I will remove from you your heart of stone and give you a heart of flesh.*

What came next was another one of those unexpected blessings, an answer to a prayer before I even knew the question. All three of the kids found their own Lego stage. Maybe it was our trip to the Lego Store at Downtown Disney, or Andrew's birthday weekend at Legoland in Carlsbad. Each now went their own direction: Andrew chose the Titanic, Kaitlyn a yacht, Jillian a little village.

These weren't group projects, but for me they became something much greater. Over several weeks, sitting side by side with each of them, the builds turned into close, meaningful time.

Those moments opened windows of insight into who they were. Picasso reportedly said at twelve he could draw like *Raphael*, but it took his whole life to learn to draw like a child. I now had a glimpse into that illusive wonder that only comes from a child's imagination.

Andrew loved opening the plastic bags and assembling the little Lego people, quickly taking charge as foreman, guiding me through the instructions while we talked and I snapped pieces into place.

Jillian and I worked like a team of engineers, dividing and conquering. She'd grab her pile, I'd grab mine, and we'd join forces at just the right moment when our builds came together. A chip off the old block, I thought.

My dynamic with Kaitlyn was entirely different. We pulled from the same pile, moving in sync, never overreaching, never colliding, developing our own shorthand: "I'm looking for a short-skinny." ... "Do you have a white elbow?" ... "Is that a square end?"

When I think back, Jarrod had his own unique way of approaching Legos. He liked to add little twists not pictured on the outside of the box, that somehow made the finished product better. More often than not, I was his hands, more helper than builder.

Reflecting years later, I realized I was always destined to "fail" at that pile left behind, without him. Jarrod wasn't an assembler; he was a creator. I like to imagine him now, watching all this new creation unfold. Smiling as his dad and sister built together, and just as happily getting to know Kaitlyn and Andrew as they played with something he loved.

NARROW FOCUS

In many ways, all the time we'd spent together pointed Erin and me toward planning a special adventure for the *Fab Five*, one that signaled our progress and would be a threshold experience.

We decided on a couple nights in a hotel at the entry of Zion National Park and devote a full day to hiking The Narrows. We had each visited the park before, but never this magnificent hike, a slot canyon carved between towering sandstone walls, where the trail is the Virgin River itself.

We'd wade through water knee-deep or higher, pushing forward as far as our will would take us, knowing that the deeper and narrower the canyon became, the more breathtaking the beauty around us would be. Our intent was to discover together.

On the night of our arrival, it turned out to be a rocky start. I dropped "Baby," the name Erin had affectionately given our favorite pocket-sized digital camera, with its autofocus button that seemed like pure magic. Up to that point, *Baby* had captured quite the highlight reel of our family adventures. Hence the name, and hence the way we normally handled it, with extreme care. Oops. That evening, while Erin and the kids settled into the hotel, I made a trip into a nearby store in search of a suitable replacement.

For our group, an "early start" meant about 8 a.m. After a simple continental breakfast at the hotel, we picked up our water boots and large wooden walking sticks from an outfitter just a short walk away. Once geared up, we were ready and excited, especially Andrew. He's the one who loves to leap off rocks at lakes and rivers. Whenever water is involved, he somehow finds it all the more enticing.

A scenic shuttle ride carried us through the park to the Riverside Walk, a paved path following the Virgin River for about a mile, with cottonwoods and willows on display. Toward the end, the canyon comes into view. We joined a group of about fifty other hikers; all apparently having placed a deposit on the same Merlin-inspired walking stick.

The trail is an immediate gateway into the river. We stepped onto slippery rocks and around large boulders as the water flowed gently, cool and refreshing, tinged with sediment that added shades of brown. Towering canyon walls soared nearly a thousand feet overhead on both sides, a dramatic reminder of how rivers carve their paths with unstoppable force. The grandeur made it easy to understand why early Mormon settlers saw this as the land of Zion, a natural sanctuary.

At this stage, the hike was comfortable, helped by a canyon breeze, with the water rising anywhere from ankle-deep to mid-calf. It was a moderate stretch. We drifted into two groups, not far apart. The kids together, and Erin and me side by side. Erin pointed out the striking rings along the canyon walls, streaked with rusty, creamy, and burnt hues, stone layers offering a window into millennia of time.

We tested out our new camera. I sent up a silent prayer that the salesperson's promise, that it had the same magic auto-focus button as Baby, was truth in advertising. To my relief, Baby 2.0 passed its first test.

When we started, the canyon stretched about eighty feet across. A few miles in, that distance had narrowed to nearly half, as the walls seemed to press in on us with each step forward. This was when our poles proved their worth. With the water rising to our knees and thighs, and higher for the kids, it took more effort to push against the current. Our footing over sand and slick rocks became increasingly tricky.

Soon after, we reached a stretch where dry ledges appeared along the canyon's edge, marked by massive boulders. The kids needed no further invitation. They scrambled up immediately, with Andrew leading the charge.

As we resumed our trek upstream, the canyon narrowed further and the water levels rose in step. We soon reached the turn-around point for our *Fab Five*. What had begun with us seeing our boots in ankle-deep water soon became a continual rise above knees, thighs and eventually water up to Andrew's waist.

That was our signal to head back. We retraced our steps downstream, laughing and triumphant. It felt like a victory march. The day's story was sealed, not just in our memories, but safely stored in Baby 2.0's memory card, the annals of our own little history preserved.

When we made it back to the hotel, it was dinner time. No rest for the ambitious hikers determined to test their limits. It was a quick call to action to get ourselves ready. Our clothes, still damp, filled with sand, and carrying rock.

That was also when it became apparent that Andrew's shoes had developed a musky odor that quickly filled the room. It was non-negotiable. Outside they went.

We had a great dinner together that night, sharing perspectives on what the experience had meant for each of us. We laughed about me slipping on a rock, about Erin refusing to let me touch the camera until trust was rebuilt, about the sprint to the rock that suddenly became a challenge of its own. We recalled Andrew pressing forward in waist-high water, the determination on his face clear as he fought to keep going.

It's these moments that reveal how special it is to play outside in nature. How easy it is to lose yourself in wild places. To feel the wonder of what lies around the next bend, hidden from view, stirring nervous excitement, where the reality of danger and demand for respect meet in perfect harmony with the beautiful reward of answering the challenge.

IN MY DAUGHTER'S EYES

It felt like we were fitting the pieces together, building something new.

The Lego creation was beginning to take shape, foundations of Jillian's village, the tailwinds of Kaitlyn's pleasure cruise, and a few icebergs dodged from Andrew's Titanic tribute. What I wasn't entirely sure of was how Jillian felt about it all, beneath the surface.

I thought back to one of Jillian's signature moves as a baby, a memory that always makes me smile. When she first started moving under her own power, her style was completely her own. Jarrod's story was written in his footed sleepers, burned holes through the knees from constant forward charges, testing every boundary, always pushing out of sight. He never had a chance. Jennifer's motherly instinct could anticipate his every move.

Jillian's approach was altogether her own, joined with a very different appetite for risk. Her innovation on the carpet came in the form of a backwards scoot, slow, deliberate, cautious, with a rear-view gaze to guide her path. Make no mistake, this wasn't inefficiency or shortcoming. It was precision. Balance. Artful and skillful. Her PJ's stayed intact, and she always reached her destination, happy even, to stay in the company of that watchful eye.

This reminded me that Jillian sometimes sees the path differently. Her approach and tempo may not always align with others, but that doesn't mean she isn't moving forward. With that in mind, I decided to take her out for a hike, just the two of us. A chance to "scoot" our way along the trail together, backing into some deeper conversations about her feelings as all these new forces built around her.

We chose Forest Falls, returning to the trailhead that led up toward Gorgonio. And no, I wasn't about to drag her up those punishing switchbacks in some cruel attempt at bending her to my will. This would be a gentle walk, along the riverbed, through the foothills, and toward the beautiful waterfall tucked into the lowlands.

It didn't take long for us to find the right timing, shifting between small chats about the scenery, the labored breaths of walking over rock, and stretches of relaxed togetherness. Jillian brought up the topic before I did, which, to me, was the perfect start.

After all, she and I had always been the ones who worked from the same pile, dividing and conquering, then coming back together for the next mission.

My role that day was to listen. This wasn't a mountain trek, but I treated it as a *Heaven Hike*, where it'd be a time to keep my mind and heart open, and my mouth buttoned up. A keen listener.

What Jillian wanted me to hear was simple but powerful. She told me how proud she was that I had found the courage to love again. How much she noticed my

119

happiness. How much she liked Erin. She talked about becoming close friends with Kaitlyn and Andrew, and how fun it had been getting to know them.

Then it was my turn. I had only one question, because by then, we already seemed to see everything the same way. *What if Erin and I were to get married?* Jillian didn't hesitate: "Dad, what are you waiting for!"

Her words were a clear and resounding reminder of why Martina McBride's, *In My Daughter's Eyes* brings my thoughts to Jillan each time I hear it, especially these lines from the song:

> *And when she wraps her hand around my finger,*
> *how it puts a smile in my heart.*
> *Everything becomes a little clearer.*
> *I realize what life is all about.*
> *It's hanging on when your heart is had enough.*
> *It's giving more when you feel like giving up.*
> *I've seen the light.*
> *It's in my daughter's eyes.*

8
LOVING GIFT

To love and be loved is to feel the sun from both sides.

—David Viscott
(How to Live with Another Person)

See! The winter is past; the rains are over and gone. Flowers appear on the earth; the season of singing has come, the cooling of doves is heard in our land.

—Song of Songs 2:11-12

And now these three remain: faith, hope and love. But the greatest of these is love.

—1 Corinthians 13:13

Love is composed of a single soul inhabiting two bodies.

—Aristotle
(Lives of Eminent Philosophers)

It was time. My heart was sealed. Convinced that Erin felt the same way, my confidence was ready to surrender my heart once more. First, it was to God that I bent my knee in desperate prayer, to put the broken pieces back together, and give me the new ones that would fit into the image of a future I could not yet see.

For me, these puzzle pieces came in the contemplative moments on the trail, on the walks I called *Heaven Hikes*. They were truths that gave me purpose and clarity, nothing short of a path to survival. But that path was also dusted with deception, the whisper of temptation and doubt, eager to celebrate my misery alongside me. When I opened the door and allowed the Holy Spirit to enter, who, it felt to me, had merely been standing by, waiting for the invitation, I was armed with a shield. The whisper of lies was no match for a thunderous truth.

In that moment, Psalms 3:3 impressed itself on me: *But you, Lord, are a shield around me, my glory, the One who lifts my head high.*

I was sustained by this growing strength, which carried me to this moment, the ultimate gift of grace and mercy. The blessing of all blessings. I had fallen in love, fully and completely.

RISING TOGETHER

At the nucleus, the loving center, was Erin. Another ring of love surrounded it, comprised of three blessings all their own, and even more so together. It wasn't long ago, I thought, that I had been surprised by a sunrise, a shameful reminder that I had given in to temptation, letting those whispered lies grow loud enough to beat me down into darkness. Now, I was watching a sunrise in all its glory.

Before the sun is even visible, its glow gently transforms the pitch dark into enough light to see, to anticipate what is coming. Life stirs in the wild. Birds burst into song; a squirrel runs up a tree with purpose. As the light grows, the sun rises into view, painting everything in color, building momentum with the sights and sounds of life awakening. A tree with broken limbs, scarred by weather or fire, reveals itself, vulnerable, yet stunning in its resilience. Nearby water reflects the sun in radiant bounces of light.

On a lake, river, or beach, daybreak greets those willing to receive the gift. A fishing boat heads out for an early start. A couple walks the pier, savoring their coffee in the salt air.

This is how sunrises are meant to be experienced, as gifts. I was ready to leave behind the curse of the sunrise I had dwelt in for far too long.

There was a strength building inside me, but it wasn't rock solid yet. Around that time, one of my favorite movies happened to be on. I caught it near the end.

For Love of the Game stars Kevin Costner as veteran pitcher Billy Chapel. Set to be his last game on the mound, *Chappy* unexpectedly finds himself on the brink of greatness, the coveted perfect game. The film weaves back and forth between his present battle on the field and flashbacks that reveal deeper meaning to what is unfolding.

Chapel had suffered what looked to be a career-ending injury to his pitching hand. Yet he was determined to persevere, showing singular focus in his return to the game he loved. Pitch after pitch, Chapel replayed his life story in his mind, drawing strength.

Chapel also had a secret, a hidden talent known only to him. He could slip into a meditative state in which the roar of the crowd and the distractions of a taunting, restless batter went completely silent. All that remained was sixty feet of distance between him and what he wanted. But the talent he had mastered had a limit, one he didn't realize until it was gone, just when he needed it the most.

It was now the end of the game, only three batters left. He was staring down either perfection, or what had become all too familiar, another loss. This is when the thunder of the crowd returned, Chapel's spell broken, the reality of the challenge fully exposed. Somehow, he had to summon strength from an unknown source.

Clutching his hand, both a painful reminder of the adversity he had overcome to reach this moment and the undeniable impediment that still threatened him, Chapel kept throwing, fueled by raw determination and not without pain.

This is when the drama reached its peak. One batter away from perfection, the opposing manager made a lineup change, sending in a rookie pinch hitter.

In no uncertain terms, he told him exactly what needed to be done: "Break it."

As the rookie stepped up, Chapel's catcher, Gus, walked out to the mound. The exchange was simple but pivotal. *Chappy* admitted he had nothing left. Gus assured him that all he needed to do was get the ball across the plate, that the team was ready to carry him the rest of the way. It wasn't all on his shoulders. They wanted the chance to share the weight and the triumph.

Of course, in classic Hollywood fashion, the next pitch resulted in an infield grounder, destined to slip through for a crushing base hit. But in slow motion, a fielder miraculously scooped it up and fired to first, just in time. Perfection achieved, despite everything that stood defiant, injury, loss, determined opposition, even the finality of knowing this was his last chance.

My absolute favorite line in the movie follows. After the final out, Vin Scully, his voice rich with the gravitas only he could deliver, says: *The cathedral that is Yankee Stadium belongs to a Chapel.*

I was drawing parallels and finding strength from the movie in all kinds of different ways. Of all the reflections that flooded in, one stood out above the rest.

I was reminded of Jillian's words of encouragement: *What are you waiting for?* I remembered outrunning the sheriff with Andrew, chasing after something we both wanted. I recalled climbing a mountain with Kaitlyn, inventing our own creative language for building something together. And I felt the warmth of Jarrod's hug, his voice speaking gently to my heart once more: *Let's go, Dad.*

My team was with me and nothing was going to "break it." I was reaching for my own sense of perfection, encouraged by the promise of sunrise and by the people who proved I wasn't alone.

NEVER DANCING ALONE

Even though we shared so many fun times together as a family, Erin and I had found our own very special loves along the way. We bonded over '80s bands, with a regular lineup of two or three concerts always on our calendar. We could be found on hiking trails together, at one of our favorite restaurants, on weekend getaways just far enough to feel like escapes, or simply on the couch for a Netflix night.

A work trip to Las Vegas was coming up, and though I was still waiting for the perfect moment, I did already have the ring. Perhaps this would be it. I've never been much of a fan of Vegas, but the event was at the Paris Hotel. While not exactly the "city of love," it did have a French restaurant I knew from professional circles to be exceptional. If Vegas is anything, it's a place that draws you into an imagined world. That weekend, we wandered from Italy to France, riding gondolas and climbing the Eiffel Tower, all without ever leaving the desert.

The moment felt right. And it was, because the answer was "Yes." Still, being down on one knee, stretching out a hand with a ring you hope is enchanting, fumbling through words you had carefully planned but that tumbled out differently in a clumsy attempt at confidence, is a nerve-wracking position to be in. It is the ultimate promise of a lifetime, made in the most vulnerable of ways. Erin stood before me with stunning beauty and poise.

Though the moment felt overwhelming in my mind, the instant our hands met her touch calmed my nerves. I knew God had brought us together as a wonderful blessing. Later, I was reminded of Genesis 2:18: *The Lord God said, "It is not good for the man to be alone. I will make a helper suitable for him."*

We did eventually make it to the actual Eiffel Tower, and there, in the romantic glow and glitz only Paris itself can offer, we celebrated as our *Fab Five*.

I am no Vin Scully, but if I were calling the moment, I might have said: *The empty promise that is Las Vegas belongs to the full hearts that said yes.*

Our wedding was a small gathering at a greenhouse in Santa Barbara, nestled between the Riviera coastline and a bird sanctuary along the bike path we often rode on weekends. The kids were amazing, each took turns with the microphone, sharing how special the wedding was to them. It wasn't planned or prompted; it just happened.

Not long after, Andrew took to the dance floor, necktie now tied around his head like the Karate Kid, full moves on display. And in my mind's eye, as clear as if under a spotlight, there was Jarrod, shuffling right alongside him. He had fashioned his tie the same way, showing Andrew, he had a partner for whatever came next.

PART IV
Finding Home

9
THE MOUNTAIN'S OFFERING

In the midst of winter, I found there was, within me, an invincible summer.

—Albert Camus
(Return to Tipasa)

You climb mountains not so the world can see you, but so you can see the world.

—David McCullough Jr.
(Commencement Speech, Wellesley High School)

Commit to the Lord whatever you do, and he will establish your plans.

—Proverbs 16:3

At first, Erin encountered *Heaven Hikes* as a supportive observer from the sidelines. My hiking routines appeared no different than going to the gym before or after work. There was no ceremony or explanation, just a couple of hours during the week, sometimes longer on weekends with an earlier start time.

I did my best to keep the hikes in balance with our life together off the trail. Erin would often comment that I returned home calmer than tired, a breath of fresh air in every sense of the expression. She noticed the discipline, the repetition, and how intentional I was about protecting what was clearly a special time, laced up in the boots.

I was careful not to hide my grief from Erin, so there were days when she knew I was carrying more weight than usual. It was on those days when I returned noticeably lighter after a hike that her curiosity deepened about what the *Heaven Hikes* meant to me.

Eventually, she asked if I'd mind a companion on the trail once in a while. By then, solitude was no longer the only path. I had come to appreciate both the lovely and lonely time the trail offered. I welcomed the opportunity to share *Heaven Hikes* with Erin, to be a guide for an up-close and honest experience of what they hold for me.

Erin's first step into *Heaven Hikes* marked a quiet turning point. What had been mostly a solitary act of faithful movement became, at times, enriching steps forward taken together. Walking alongside one another didn't dilute the purpose; it deepened it. In moving together, support didn't need to be spoken, and understanding didn't need translation.

One of my fondest memories of walking with Erin was in Vancouver, British Columbia. It was an outdoor adventure all its own, with some familiar nature we'd come to love at home. North Vancouver shared the gift of coastal mountains with Santa Barbara, both distinct in their own ways and unforgettable. In SB, several breathtaking trails and vistas along those mountain edges were our favorite *Heaven Hikes* together.

I had been spending a lot of time in Vancouver for work, and had discovered the Grouse Grind. It's just short of two miles, but it's not the distance that makes it a trial. It's the relentless climb, roughly 2,600 feet of elevation gain from start to finish. Its nickname says it all: "Mother Nature's Stairmaster."

The only forgiving part of the hike is that it's one-way up. The ride down is by gondola, with the bonus of a free ticket if you climb rather than ride up. It takes about two hours to conquer its reported 2,830 steps, and at times, you're even using your hands.

I quickly fell in love with the Grind. Early that summer, with daylight stretching until around 9:00 p.m., I found I could fit it in at least once a week. At the top, near the gondola station, is a standout restaurant, always a worthy reward after earning my way up the hard way.

A couple of months later, I doubled up my weeks in Vancouver on purpose, making space so Erin could join me for a week with a clear schedule and free time. We took the

Amtrak from Sacramento to Seattle and then drove across the border, making the trip itself part of the adventure.

We still laugh about our private sleeper car, not large enough for two people side by side, which meant I was relegated to the top bunk, held in place by netting hooked from one side. I had no idea trains speed up at night. Up there, with just a few inches between my face and the ceiling, it turned into a bone-rattling ride I'll never forget.

Once there, we biked through Stanley Park, took the ferry, and stayed overnight at the Empress on Victoria Island. Midway through the trip, unplanned, Erin expressed that she wanted to give the Grind a try. I knew it'd be a stretch but that she could do it.

TREE BY TREE

Vancouver stays cool in the summer. The north side of Grouse had a misty chill in the morning air. We stepped onto "Mother Nature's Stairmaster" and began climbing. This isn't the kind of trail with winding switchbacks, distant views, or scenic lookouts along the way. It's simply facing the mountain and walking straight up through a rainforest thick with cedar and Douglas fir.

We kept a respectable pace for the first 500 steps, soon encountering the trail's features, stone steps and dirt embankments carved into the mountainside to guide the way upward. We reached our first milestone, a sign marked ¼, indicating a quarter of the climb was behind us.

Erin was visibly slowing down. We paused for a break and reminded ourselves there was no rush. If it took four hours instead of two, so be it. We had water, time, and no need to treat it like a time trial. The Grouse Grind does keep official times for those who care to compete for bragging rights, but none of that interested us.

Not long after, we came across some fallen timber that Forest Service had fashioned into a rugged but inviting bench. We caught our breath, rehydrated, and admired the beauty of the mountain. The cool air was refreshing, and we marveled at Vancouver itself. It truly is an outdoor play-ground.

We pressed on, step by step, reaching the halfway mark, then the three-quarter point. That's when Erin hit the wall. She leaned heavily against the trunk of a tall cedar, the tree practically holding her up. We stood there together, wanting to make it but the strain was undeniable. We could always turn back, the route down was far easier than the grind upward.

Several runners flew past us, clearly on timed ascents for leaderboard glory. After that, I suggested we turn back and sooner enjoy a restaurant I had discovered on a previous trip, a converted country cottage with a veranda and garden seating. To my surprise, Erin wanted to continue. We made a new plan, take the steps from one chosen tree to the next, pause, then repeat.

It worked. Rounding a corner into an abrupt clearing was indication that we'd made it. Another runner passed us, casually mentioning it was his *second* climb of the day. We laughed again.

The Grouse Grind would stand as our greatest hiking challenge together, a memory I deeply cherish. And thankfully, when we both look back, it's the laughter we remember, not the arguments our legs and feet had along the way.

Although Erin was gracious about the Grind, she made it clear that while the most demanding trail and bike challenges would be mine alone, she wanted to remain part of the journey, joining the slower, gentler outings and offering her encouragement nearby when the path went beyond her comfort zone.

The tougher stretches would be solo but the experience still made room for both of us. Those adventures turned into weekend getaways that blended solo challenges with time together, built around a cozy B&B and the hunt for a rare gem of a restaurant that fed our shared culinary passion.

SIX MORE FORGED

The following summer, I mapped out a new *Heaven Hikes* challenge. This time, it wouldn't be a curated series of suggested hikes. I handpicked five, plus a sixth that offered two summits, seven peaks in all, each over 8,000 feet. They included Mt. Whitney, Half Dome, Mt. Pinos with Sawmill Mountain, the "Cactus to Clouds" ascent back to San Jacinto, and two Tahoe peaks at that year's camp, Freel and Heavenly.

Unlike the last challenge, some of these climbs I would take on alone, others with friends.

Like Chapel, I'd become adept at finding quietude, even while sharing trails with others. It opened me to the best of both solitude and companionship. God was reshaping me in ways that not only drew me closer to Jarrod, but to others as well. Proverbs 27:17 reminded me: *As iron sharpens iron, so one person sharpens another.*

STONE HAMMOCK

The first hike in my next adventure challenge would be Half Dome, a test in every sense. The plan was for my friend Nick and me to start a day early, camping overnight at Little Yosemite Valley near the approach, and then meet a few other friends on the summit the following day. From there, we'd all descend together to the Happy Isles trailhead.

Half Dome rises to about 8,839 feet. The route meant about four miles the first day, then another eight the second, with a total vertical gain of nearly 4,800 feet. The hike itself is strenuous, but the real test comes in the final 400 feet: pulling yourself up cables, unharnessed, over slick granite, walking from plank to plank in a straight line with other hikers.

Permits in hand, Nick and I grabbed lunch at the trailhead café before starting out. I had definitely stepped up my game from the "Six Pack." Not that those hikes were easy, but Half Dome offered another level of majesty.

I wasn't following in Alex Honnold's free-solo footsteps, but I understood what he meant on *60 Minutes* when he described Half Dome as "a smooth wall of rock, a nearly vertical granite slab... and so you're really trusting the rubber on your shoes."

That challenge would wait until tomorrow. For now, we followed the trail past two of Yosemite's iconic waterfalls, including Nevada Falls, nearly 600 feet high. It was a steep but beautiful hike to camp. Rain began just as we arrived, so we quickly set up our tents and ducked inside.

It was dark by the time it stopped. Nick and I hung out briefly, but we were both tired from the day's climb with heavy packs and eager for an early start. We wanted to reach the cables before the crowds.

Inside my tent, I pulled out a pocket Bible I always traveled with; there was always room for it in my pack. Theodore Roosevelt once described camping in Yosemite as "like lying in a great solemn cathedral, far vaster and more beautiful than any built by the hand of man." That night my sanctuary was humbler, zipped in to stay dry, flashlight and Bible in hand. Still, I nodded in agreement with TR.

I had probably only been asleep an hour when uninvited guests arrived. Black bears. They were scavenging, prying at the bear boxes where we had locked away our food. The snorts, the clanging of metal lids, and the cracking of sticks was a racket I wasn't going to sleep through. And then I remembered, with a jolt, that I had a half-eaten Clif Bar at my feet inside the tent. I grabbed it just as one of the bears slammed into that very corner. Thankfully, the tent held, and he didn't circle back for another pass. After a tense few minutes, the bears moved on, leaving me wide awake, grateful for bear boxes, and nylon walls that somehow held their ground.

I was out of the tent by sunrise. Nick was already walking back from the Merced River, where he'd gathered water for coffee. Nick worked at REI, so he had all the best lightweight gear and gadgetry, and I was benefiting. A hot cup of coffee to start a long day ahead was perfect. Afterward, we both returned to the river, treated more water, and filled the bladders in our packs. We were ready to move.

We hiked through the forest, passed alongside a creek, and climbed a granite shoulder that brought us to the Subdome. The switchbacks here were steeper, cut directly into the granite slabs, demanding more effort with every step.

Soon, the trail broke open onto an exposed point. From there, we could see the sheer east face of Half Dome. The cables themselves weren't visible yet, but tiny figures inching upward in the distance gave scale to what lay ahead.

This was the moment I wasn't sure about. The hike, yes, I was ready for that. But the cables? I had watched plenty of YouTube videos of people climbing them, yet none of that meant anything compared to standing here in person, staring up at the awesome sight of what I was about to attempt.

The fear that set in at that moment was almost enough to make me stand aside, cheer Nick on, and wait for him to return. But I said a silent prayer and thought of Jarrod on my back.

My mind drifted to Erin on Grouse in Vancouver. I decided I would take it one wooden plank at a time, never looking down, saving that for the return. *Astra Petamus!* I was on my way up, sticking to the plan.

Nick ascended as expected, swiftly and deliberately. I moved more cautiously, but soon found a tempo, a rhythm of grab-and-step that carried me upward. I channeled Erin's "tree-to-tree" method from Grouse Mountain, and it worked. When I finally stepped onto the sprawling summit of Half Dome, it was amazing.

Part of the exhilaration was adrenaline, overcoming fear, finding my footing. But more than that, it was the view itself, the reality of being up there.

Nick immediately headed to the slightly higher spot to claim the summit. I walked the other way, to a more secluded spot, dropped my pack, and lay down. One leg crossed over the other, hands behind my head, resting on the edge of my pack, heaven surrounding me in every direction.

By then, I had learned that each *Heaven Hike* tested me differently and revealed something new. This one didn't carry me back to a memory of Jarrod from a different season; it carried me forward, into a place with him for the first time.

I could sense Jarrod with me, almost as if he were a teenager and we had climbed Half Dome together. It was a new kind of closeness, imagining him not only in memory but in the present. I lay there in solitude, but not alone.

Without me noticing, Nick snapped a photo. Like that moment stretched out on San Jacinto, this was my hammock-at-the-beach pose. But the backdrop wasn't crashing waves or sand. I was on rock.

This wasn't Buffett's *Margaritaville*. It was something sobering and breathtaking, an entirely different kind of beauty.

FEELING NUTTY

Years earlier, long before hiking mountains was even a thought, let alone a quest of my own, a business colleague once described to me the experience of standing atop Whitney. As he told it, I could see it was a moment of pride for him. But at the time, his description of the physical challenge struck me as almost beyond comprehension.

That was a season when my focus was consumed by career. I was traveling the world, poorly balancing work and life, with my eyes fixed more on the prize glimmering from each rung of the corporate ladder than on any true summit, even one as brilliant as Whitney.

Muir famously said that men ascend mountains as instinctively as squirrels ascend trees. My inner squirrel was late to the party, but with permit in hand and a growing résumé of mountain hikes worn into my boots, I felt nutty enough to go for it.

Conditioning and will could carry me only one place, as high as my capabilities would take me, on my own heavenly mission. That place was the summit of Mt. Whitney. At 14,505 feet, the highest point in the Sierra Nevada, the tallest peak in the lower 48, where my head would literally be in the clouds.

Words of inspiration reached me in a passage describing the mountain of the Lord's temple rising above all others, exalted beyond the hills, a place to which people would be drawn (Micah 4:1).

Boots on, pack cinched, and my personal hiker's prayer, with an intimate call to *Astra Petamus*, I left the Jeep behind. It was 2:00 a.m., pitch dark.

Headlamp on, I stepped forward. The trailhead already sat at over 8,300 feet; higher than many summits I was used to reaching after a full day's climb. The intimate scent of pine reminded me where I was, and of the special day ahead.

This was my first true pre-dawn hike, and it felt adventurous from the first steps. Nobody in sight, just me walking into a mountain under a dimly lit trail, the moon and stars doing their best to stretch the horizon. Overhead, the Milky Way blazed across the sky, a reminder of where this whole journey began, with that "special hiker named Jarrod."

The opening switchbacks rose expectedly, but my legs surprised me by waking up ahead of schedule. Off to a good start, I thought. Shuffling my poles, thoughts of Jarrod already with me, I threw in a little foot shuffle of my own, LMFAO-style, an inside joke for him on this early wake-up call. If anyone had come up behind me, they would've caught me mid-dance, but thankfully it stayed my own private laugh.

And with that, my mind flashed back to my favorite decade, the '80s, and one of its quirky TV comedies, *The Greatest American Hero*. The story was simple, a superpowered suit from outer space handed to an ordinary high-school teacher and left for him to figure out. He never quite did, and the crash-landings became his calling card. It wasn't a particular episode that came to me that morning, but the theme song.

As the trail wound upward and the stars glowed above, the lyrics carried me forward:

> *Believe it or not, I'm walkin' on air.*
> *I never thought I could feel so free.*
> *Flyin' away on a wing and a pray'r.*
> *Who could it be?*
> *Believe it or not, it's just me.*

Not exactly a battle cry I'd share with too many people, but it felt perfect that day, one Jarrod would have appreciated, and reminded me was absolutely dumb, though secretly loved. I didn't yet realize there'd be challenges ahead that would call for superhuman abilities, or at least stretch me to my limits.

The headlamp wasn't my only new REI purchase. For the first time, I'd get to use crampons over late-winter remnants of snow and ice. It brought me back to that "diamondback" mindset, focused, calm, sharp. As reflective, inspiring, and peaceful as wild places are, they also demand constant awareness, with instincts primed and ready.

The sun was rising, and mountain sunrises had become a central part of my journey. Somehow, I had timed it perfectly. The forest opened as the trail wound beside Mirror Lake. The lake lived up to its name. As the sun crested, the reflection sharpened, peaks above greeting their partner below. The lake offered back a silver shadow of gratitude against the snow-covered granite, a special exchange, like overhearing a private moment between two old friends.

Leaving the trees behind, I climbed into rougher terrain. Soon the stage revealed Mt. Whitney itself, and within view, the sight I knew was coming, but far more intimidating in person than in any picture or video. The infamous *99 switchbacks.*

They clawed up to Trail Crest at 13,700 feet, earned after 1,700 vertical feet in just 2 miles. Almost a Grouse Grind by itself. And this after seven hours of hiking and nearly 4,000 feet already climbed. I tipped my hat in memory of the guy who waved at Erin and me on his *second* Grind while we were gassed trying to finish just once.

As I sized up the switchbacks, a helicopter caught my eye, perched skillfully on a large boulder not far away. Later I'd learn it was a rescue for a climber who had slid off one of the higher rocks. It seemed off-route, but some climbers cut their own lines here, testing themselves or seeking shortcuts. More often than not, those choices add unnecessary danger to the hike's already nonnegotiable hazards.

A few minutes later, I found myself both making a quick trail friend and tapping into my own Boy Scout preparedness.

"Friend" is loosely given. There was probably an introduction, but trail encounters aren't the same as meeting a random sports fan at a pub. Hiking interaction carries a different weight. A blend of shared suffering and joy, wrapped in the pleasant disbelief that someone else is willing to take on the same challenge.

He was younger than me, mid-twenties. At first, I was surprised he had made it this far. No boots, just trekking sandals. A thin windbreaker. Meanwhile, temperatures were dropping as we pushed higher into snow. I was already feeling the cold through my layers, though I had a puffer that carried more punch than the standard weekend Patagonia.

We walked together for a bit. He was chatty, which was fine. I'd been working on opening more space for others, and it's not in my nature to be off-putting, more inclined to let others enjoy themselves even if quietness is my first choice.

We made it as far as exchanging the early get-to-know you stuff, learning we both grew up in SoCal's Orange County, when he suddenly lost his footing. He caught his fall with his hand, but sliced it on the sharp granite. Now he was bleeding, a little shocked. It wasn't serious, thankfully.

I reached into my pack. From the start of my hiking days, I'd always carried a zip bag of first-aid basics. Neosporin, bandages, the simple stuff. I cleaned him up, patched the cut, and we kept going. Not as much talking after that, but still, it was good to have some company on the trail. Together, we were now approaching the switchbacks.

Starting over shale and wide, the switchbacks quickly tightened, climbing relentlessly, end to end, only to reverse and start again. Who engineered switchbacks, anyway? Inspired by Roman ingenuity, or the cruel humor of someone determined to cover their tracks, I wondered.

We pushed on and reached the cables section, with chain-assisted handholds that reminded me of the Devil's Backbone and Half Dome. That part was manageable, but what came next was questionable. Ahead lay an ice crossing, a bottleneck where the trail vanished into a sheer gap glazed with snow and ice. On either side were drops I didn't want to measure.

I watched others carefully pick their way across, a few strapping on crampons for the first time. My thinking? This is too much. What am I doing? I'm about to literally jump a slick obstacle just to get to the other side, knowing I'll face it again later, more tired, testing my luck a second time. That's when my mind went to Jarrod.

COURAGE ON THE CREST

After school, his ritual was to flop onto the couch, pull on his headset, mic in place, and light up the screen with *Call of Duty*. He was good. I tried playing with him a few times, but it was always a disaster. He laughed at my clumsy efforts, which I didn't mind.

My childhood "gaming" was an Atari 2600 with a joystick and a single red button, competing for baseball cards or quarters over *Mario Bros*...the original.

I didn't have the reflexes, or the appetite, to join him in a firefight with strangers across the world, some of them experts. Jarrod, though, kept pace with adults and college kids, holding his own in missions that sounded to me like tactical operations.

Sometimes I'd just sit in amazement as he navigated impossible setups with ease. I'd hear the curses of his opponents, and then the praise of teammates: *Nice one! You're on fire, let's go.* It was surreal. The same kid who wouldn't hurt a wasp was suddenly a respected squadmate, leading the charge in a virtual warzone.

And then there was the time Jarrod, either caught in the thrill of a hard-fought win or emboldened by the camaraderie, let out a triumphant cry through his mic. It came across spot on, until his voice betrayed him. Clearly and unmistakably sounding his age.

The reaction was immediate. *You're a kid.* One by one: drop, drop, drop. His squad abandoned him, likely the responsible thing, I suppose. A small parental check-in moment for me, watching it all unfold, without objection.

But Jarrod didn't flinch. He peeled off the headset, completely unfazed, tossed the controller aside, and hopped on his scooter. Just like that, he was onto the next adventure.

Crampons in place, I decided to channel that warrior mentality Jarrod had once shown me. This was my chance to prove that Dad had some moves too, fit for a difficult playing field.

I jumped the three-foot ice gap, spikes catching as they bit into the granite on the other side. Feeling momentarily cavalier, I threw a hang loose sign to my trail buddy.

He was next. No crampons. Just a free jump, all smiles. Two thoughts came to mind. One, I'd completely overthought the whole thing. Two, I didn't have nearly enough first aid in my pack.

We kept climbing, up and over, back and forth, as the switchbacks slowly surrendered. At last, the views opened wide, revealing Sequoia National Park, jagged silhouettes, sprawling basins, endless ridgelines across the Sierra.

Trail Crest stood at 13,700 feet, Whitney's summit only about 850 feet higher. I could see it clearly now, people walking toward it. It was within reach.

It had taken ten hours to get here. I wasn't fully spent, but every hiker knows the rule. You must save enough for the return. You can leave it all on the mountain, but not too soon. Descents can be deceiving, when fatigue sets in, ankles twist, knees buckle, and focus slips. I wasn't there yet. I still had fuel in the tank. And I could feel Jarrod at my back, urging me on. Then came the unexpected.

Ahead, between Trail Crest and the traverse toward the summit, was another ice crossing, higher, slicker, and far less forgiving. My stomach sank. I thought, I don't know about this one. I've already got to renegotiate the first ice patch on the way back, and I'm pretty sure it's going to charge me a higher toll. And it was colder now, the wind cutting sharp.

While I was processing it all, my trail companion blew by, windbreaker flapping, trekking sandals flying. With grace, he leapt the ice and carried on, unhindered.

It was just after 1:00 p.m., and that's when Whitney made its move. The mountain is famous for creating its own weather; its warm air rising, slamming into the granite wall, condensing into clouds. The clouds aren't the problem. The storms they bring are. Lightning. Thunder. Hail. Snow.

WHEN THE MOUNTAIN SPEAKS

Jarrod's voice, Gene Kranz's "failure is not an option," even that Tahoe ice cream shop stranger's reminder that goals are more deliberate than wishes, all of them urged me forward. The song floated back... *flying away on a wing and a prayer*. But before my leap, the mountain, maybe God himself, spoke.

We've all heard thunder. Felt it shake a windowpane. Seen it split the night sky in brilliance. But this, this was at nearly 14,000 feet. The roar was so loud and violent it dropped me to my knees. For a second, I didn't know if it was the earth trembling or my own heart commanding my legs to bow in reverence to such raw power.

The decision was made. The mountain was asserting its authority. Hail began to fall. Reality set in. I still needed hours to descend the switchbacks, then retrace miles more down to safety. Whitney had placed a firm "closed" sign in its window. Around me, others were reaching the same conclusion. We turned back, beginning the long retreat.

Any disappointment was overshadowed by clarity. I needed to get off this mountain. My trail friend pressed on, closing the distance as he disappeared toward the summit, still throwing caution into the wind. I could only hope the stone shelter at the top would protect him and the others left with no choice but to wait it out.

Meanwhile, I pressed briskly down the switchbacks, thunder rumbling and lightning flashing in the distance. At the first ice crossing, slush from hail and snow had pooled across the ledge. I followed the lead of a couple ahead of me and just free-jumped it, no crampons this time. Time to keep moving.

Snow was now packed along the very edge of the trail where my OC friend had cut his hand earlier. I fitted the snow baskets onto my trekking poles for better grip. That's when it happened.

I lost my footing on a steep, slick edge, exposed to a drop. Instinct took over, powered more by adrenaline than skill. I drove one pole into the snow with everything I had, anchoring myself just enough to stop the slide. The other pole flew from my hand and disappeared down the mountain. Gone. I carried on with the one that remained, bent but usable.

Snow thickened and fell forcefully. I wound down carefully, switchback after switchback, finally reaching

Mirror Lake again. By then, the snow had turned to slushy rain. I hadn't packed a rain layer, note to self for next time.

Lower on the trail, I passed hikers heading up to camp, their fresh energy a stark contrast to my soaked fatigue. But by then, I'd made it out of the danger zone. My pace persisted, and after fourteen hours, I finally trudged back to Whitney Portal.

It was 4 p.m. I was drenched, exhausted, and emptied of adrenaline, the crash into reality setting in.

Back in the Jeep, I sat motionless for several minutes, heater blasting, trying to thaw. My mind replayed the thunderous moment I'd been brought to my knees before Whitney's majesty, and how close I had been. Trail Crest was the highest I had ever reached. But was this about elevation? Was my ego pushing me to prove something, perhaps to that stranger in Tahoe, or to myself?

As my hands warmed and my thoughts cleared, I realized the summit wasn't what truly mattered. I had already learned on these *Heaven Hikes* that it wasn't the height that opened the mind and connected the heart. It was the serenity. The mindfulness. The willingness to be open, to God, to Jarrod, to whatever lessons the mountain wanted to give.

That night, I checked into a modest hotel in Lone Pine. Dinner was a Superstar with cheese from Carl's Jr., but in that moment, it felt like a feast. The hot soak in the tub might as well have been the Ritz-Carlton spa.

As I eased back into comfort, I couldn't help but worry about my trail companion in sandals. I'd never see him again, but I hoped he made it to the summit, and safely back. With humility, I even congratulated him in my mind. I didn't know why he was on that mountain, but it was clear it mattered to him. His determination spoke intent.

For me, I had found enough. I'd pushed hard, risked plenty, and still walked away with the lesson Whitney wanted me to carry, that *Heaven Hikes* aren't about conquest or vanity. They're about presence, purpose, and grace, even when you're limping with one bent pole, sore-legged, and later clutching a drive-thru burger.

Philippians 3:14 ringing true in the moment: *I press on toward the goal to win the prize for which God has called me heavenward in Christ Jesus.*

I had the feeling this wasn't my last visit to Whitney. There'd be other opportunities. Meanwhile, I'd embrace the words of Eddie Cantor. His message that, "it takes twenty years to become an overnight success" ... calling attention to staying grounded in the journey, rather than expecting immediate results.

WALKING THE ANCIENT WAY

This six-pack challenge was on a tight schedule, so I was back in the boots that same month. This time it wasn't far from Santa Barbara, a double-peaked *Heaven Hike*, Mt. Pinos and Sawmill Mountain, each rising around 8,800 feet. Two county high points, Pinos above Ventura, Sawmill overseeing Kern. Both sit in the San Emigdio Range within Los Padres National Forest.

These trails wind through the Chumash Wilderness, where it's believed the summit of Pinos marks the center of the universe, a spiritual axis balancing harmony and the cosmos. Even the piñon harvest of pine nuts was considered a generous gift from nature.

It didn't take long to reach the Nordic Base trailhead and get started. The first peak is only a couple of miles in, shaded and pleasant, a moderate grade compared to the staircases I'd been climbing of late.

It's about 550 feet of gain, but being up near 9,000 feet ushers in the kind of reward I usually earn with much more effort. The out-and-back is still about seven miles, enough of a burn in the legs to declutter the mind.

It was one of those hikes where I had the trail entirely to myself. And this was one that drew thoughts of me and Jarrod, not just the past, but the present, even the future.

That was becoming more common now with these *Heaven Hikes*. I had mixed feelings about it. My greatest fear was somehow forgetting memories of him. In the months following our loss of Jarrod, I obsessively journaled every thought, every day of his life that I could recall, intent on losing none of them. More often now, though, I imagined him at his current age, not the eight-year-old boy I knew in the flesh.

It was starting to feel like a different kind of gift. Remembering those precious memories I'd shared with Jarrod in person was a treasure, but now it seemed I was becoming close to him in new ways. It truly felt as though I saw and felt him, not a physical embrace, but one that did feel warmly close.

Could this be God's love breathed into His promise in 2 Corinthians 5:8: ...*away from the body and at home with the Lord?*

I pictured Jarrod as though he were sixteen, the teenager he would have been if we were hiking this trail together and I was still wearing that automatic watch that hadn't stopped more than eight years earlier.

We'd be talking about dreams of him being noticed by some girl named Becky or Summer. Silent insecurities he wouldn't have to mention; I'd recognize them instantly.

I'd see everything in him that he couldn't yet see himself. A growing young man on his way to greatness, any blemish or hollow feeling soon to be outshone by a beauty within, certain to draw admiration beyond his wildest dreams.

My thoughts drifted to a film I'd recently watched starring Martin Sheen, *The Way*. It follows a father's journey to finish what his son had started but tragically couldn't complete. The pilgrimage to the legendary resting place of the Apostle James, known as the *Camino de Santiago*. Not a day hike; this is a five-hundred-mile walk across Spain that takes more than a month to complete.

Sheen's character makes the pilgrimage carrying a box of ashes, privately leaving some along the route, intent on walking with his son and finishing what had been his dream.

Though the story is tragic, it spoke to me as something more inspirational than sad. A father had lost his son. He carried regrets, wondering if he should have been there with him, set work aside, and reclaimed the zest for adventure he once knew but long traded for other things.

Perhaps he should have encouraged his son's journey rather than questioning it.

Yet now, walking in a foreign land, nothing else mattered. He was carrying his son with him, on a quest for discovery, to see the world through his son's eyes and, maybe, find his own way.

One of my favorite actors, Andrew McCarthy, later wrote about his own experience walking the Camino with his teenage son, Sam. He'd been so moved by the pilgrimage years earlier, when he walked it alone, that he wanted to return and share it with his son.

My own thoughts began setting a vision toward a future *Heaven Hike*, across those sacred steps, away from what's behind, focused on a purposeful walk toward something newly experienced, privately felt yet shared. A father who had lost his way, and a son just beginning to find his. Together, somehow crossing paths, present for one another, for all the wonder that may come. Discoveries not collected at the destination, but revelations received along the walk itself.

Lost in my thoughts, it wasn't long before I reached the first of the day's peaks. The broad plateau marking the summit of Mt. Pinos held a small sign and a cairn, much like the one I'd seen in San Bernardino. But my thoughts of the future weren't finished as I looked out across the panorama of the San Joaquin Valley. Someday, maybe, I thought.

A reflection from Jeremiah 6:16 stayed with me even longer than the trail itself:

Stand at the crossroads and look; ask for the ancient paths, ask where the good way is, and walk in it, and you will find rest for your souls...."

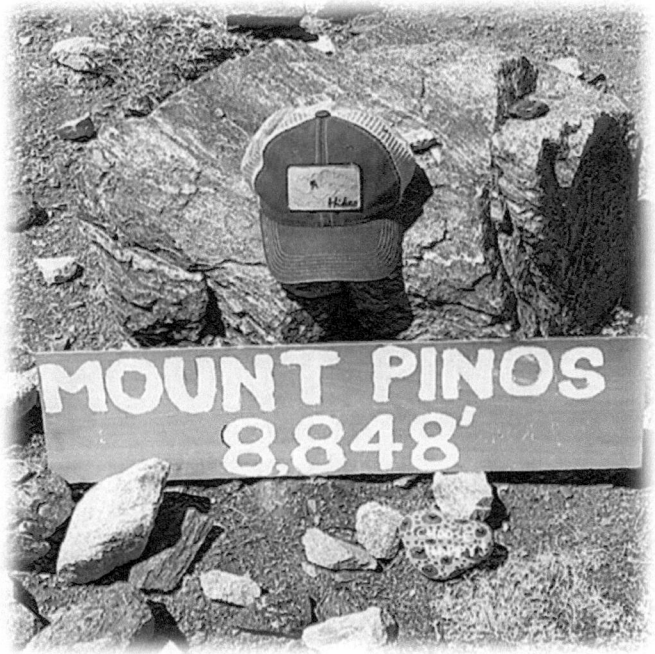

With a spring in my step, I continued on, two miles farther to Sawmill Mountain. A short distance, but one that promised to give more than it asked in return. Passing the Chumash Wilderness sign felt like an invitation to enter someplace sacred. The path opened into the welcoming sights of manzanita, lupine, and tall Jeffrey pines. The air was cool and refreshing, brushed by a gentle breeze.

I was walking the same path the Chumash believed joined sky and earth. And though I wasn't far from where I'd started, it felt as though I'd been transported someplace much farther away.

The final stretch turned rockier, but the forest stayed thick. The unassuming summit came into view, marked by a simple wooden structure known as a Chumash Spirit Tower. I rested a pinecone beside it, snapped a picture, and sat for a while to take it all in, two different gateways, close to each other, yet each significant in its own right.

SPEAKING FREELY

It was another August in Tahoe, a weeklong church camp I looked forward to all year. We had the same full itinerary of outdoor fun planned, some low-key, like a dinner cruise on a large paddle-wheeler, and others more adventurous.

By now, it was a well-oiled routine that balanced time together with our own side adventures. For me, that usually meant hiking or biking. This time, the hiking boots won the coin toss.

My second Six-Pack of Peaks was in full swing, having finished Half Dome, earned a passing grade at Trail Crest on Whitney, and checked off the double summit of Pinos and Sawmill. What remained were two within reach here in Tahoe, Freel and Heavenly. First up was Freel, intended to be a solo trek.

Freel, an offshoot of the Sierra Nevada and the high point of the Carson Range, rises to over 10,800 feet, the tallest mountain in the Tahoe Basin. It promised views of Big Blue from a vantage like no other. The route would run roughly 11 miles out and back, with about 3,000 feet of vertical gain. A strenuous day ahead, but sure to be awesome.

I found the trailhead off Willow Creek Road, not easy to locate, and parked. Following my readiness protocol, I set off on an uphill walk, through dense forest terrain.

Although planned to be a "lone and lovely" *Heaven Hike* this time, before long there'd be two of us with a shared purpose. What began as mutual uncertainty about the trail's direction turned into that signature conversation between hikers. He was quick to share his story, recovering from an ankle injury, hiking again in custom-made boots after surgery, clearly excited just to be out here. I kept what was driving me closer to the vest. "Just chasing the bucket list," I said, while the family had other plans at camp.

I've always found it difficult to reveal that part of myself. Of course, I'm proud to share the mission of *Heaven Hikes*, but whether out of reluctance to carry on a longer story or insecurity about how it might be received, it's often easier to deflect. Over the years, that hesitation has softened, a heartfelt blessing born of wishing the same healing for others. As it turned out, on this day, God joined the two of us, different injuries, both tested in the high country.

We'd spend the next several hours getting to know each other, both opening up much more. For me, that meant explaining *Heaven Hikes*, introducing Jarrod Jr., and sharing how Tahoe fits. Despite my initial caution, I found strength without asking. A whisper from Exodus 4:12: *Now go; I will help you speak and will teach you what to say.*

Our conversation settled us into an unbroken exchange. Soon we crossed through a meadow into the saddle, where we were exposed and high enough now to see scattered patches of snow. Visible in the distance were Jobs Peak and Jobs Sister, often added to Freel as a same-day trifecta, tempting detours not in the plan today.

We made our way across snowmelt and rugged footing, our horizon a sea of ridgelines more than lake views, as if transported somewhere far from Big Blue's sunlit south shore.

The wind picked up as we climbed out of Freel Pass, pushing over sand and gravel toward the final ascent. We again put our heads together to find the best route. It wasn't entirely clear, but we reasoned correctly. By the final stretch, each step sinking into loose grit, lungs heavy, I looked up as my boots carried me onto the summit of Freel.

I was awestricken by the view. Lake Tahoe spread below in a 360-degree panorama, end to end, shimmering beneath the sun.

Nearly 11,000 feet above its surface, I couldn't see a single boat or wake. Surely the lake below was buzzing with people, but from this elevation I saw it for what it truly was, glorious in its purest form.

At the summit, a metal box held a small notebook and pen. My trail buddy wrote something like: *Back in the boots, ankle be damned.* I added what had become my usual mark at this point: *Heaven Hike for Jarrod Jr.*

Looking back, it was relatable to Sheen's character in *The Way*, leaving a trace, a message, a sign that my son had been here too.

That was the end of our camaraderie on the trail. A simple "Take care, it's been fun" left us each on our own for the descent. We were headed to the same place, so it wasn't as if we vanished from each other's view immediately, but our pace naturally drifted apart. His ankle might have been showing signs of pushback, since I moved ahead, though there wasn't much left in my tank either.

When I finally reached the bottom, I thought I'd arrived where I started. But it wasn't. The wooded path I'd taken down opened into a wide meadow. I remembered a dustier entrance. Looking around, it seemed right enough, one side of the meadow faded into thick, shoulder-high vegetation; the other was walled off by a treeline extending from the forest trail I'd just come down.

Oh no, I thought. *Sorry, Jillian.* It took a while for it to sink in, but I was hopelessly lost in the wilderness. In the fog of fatigue from a long, high-altitude day, I pushed deeper into the meadow, only to realize it led nowhere and offered no clear path through. So, I turned back up the forest trail before stopping to think. *That can't be right either,* I reasoned, heading back toward where I'd just come from. The thought of retracing steps to some unknown point for an unmarked turnoff that might not even exist seemed risky, likely to make things worse.

So, I went back down into the meadow. Of course, there was no signal on my phone. I'd already made a mental note to invest in some GPS-enabled tech on my next stop at REI, but that wasn't much help in the moment. I walked in the opposite direction of the overgrown brush, past the treeline that had blocked my view. A few more steps, and there it was, the dirt road I'd seen that morning, leading back to the trailhead where it had all begun.

Relief washed over me. A humble reminder of how quickly fatigue and wilderness can tangle. Then came the laugh, at myself, for thinking that walking straight through thick brush was going to lead anywhere good. Back to Mighty Lite. I decided to leave this part of the story out of the campfire recap that night and just be thankful.

FRAMES ACROSS TIME

A couple of days after Freel, I was ready to hit the trails again. This time accompanied by a longtime friend. Erin's cousin Dillon had made a day hike of Mt. Tallac every day that week and was looking for a change of pace, if not scenery. I expected he'd leave me in the dust, but figured until that point, we'd have time to chat and catch up. Already named *Heavenly*, its billing was reassuring; it sounded like the kind of playground I was looking for. Reaching just over 10,000 feet to Monument Peak, atop what's more famously known as a winter wonderland and ski paradise, the hike would take about four hours.

We started up a wide gravel service road, zigzagging along the slope, not singletrack, but still carrying the feel of switchbacks gradually guiding us uphill. Between our conversations and the harmony of simply walking together, my mind drifted to bowling. Andrew and I had joined an adult/junior league, a four-person team, that included his friend, and his mom, the other adult. We thoughtfully named ourselves *The Whippersnappers*. We were actually doing well, a competitive little foursome.

I'd been working with Andrew, and like the afternoon he took to the fly rod so naturally, he was a quick study with a bowling hook. Most of his friends were still playing pinball on the lanes, using bumpers or rolling the ball off in that two-handed shuffle that had somehow become trendy, even at the pro level.

I wasn't a stickler, but I was old-school nonetheless, so I encouraged Andrew to learn the traditional release, rolling out from the middle and ring fingers, with the thumb in for the ride to provide lift at the release point. He was catching on, and his friends were starting to take notice.

The league hosted a doubles tournament a few weeks before this Tahoe trip, and we dominated. My competitive spirit emerged from a deeply-rooted but long-forgotten place. Four scratch games over 200, with Andrew consistently adding scores above 150.

It was a flashback to the same tournament format that Jarrod and I had played years earlier. There I was, reliving a moment with Andrew, who was about the same age Jarrod had been at the time. It didn't feel like coincidence, more like a gift. Maybe that's why my bowling rose to the moment; I didn't want to show Andrew anything but my best.

I even taught him a bit of flair, a throwback to my own youth on the Junior Amateur Tour, where a few of us more flamboyant bowlers would mimic pulling the cord of a chainsaw to signal the ball sawing through the pins when a full rack crashed into the pit. Mixed reviews from behind the scenes that day, but we were having fun.

The bowling center of Jarrod and Jillian's youth was Canyon Lanes. Once a week, that meant homework was done in the back behind the lanes. It was a casino bowling center. Management had always hoped for a bustling junior program, but the lanes stayed busy enough with seniors, members of the Morongo Band of Mission Indians, and travelers passing through.

In Jarrod's honor, Jennifer and I started an annual bowling tournament in his name. It felt like the perfect way to bring kids closer to a sport Jarrod loved and to shine a spotlight on his memory. It didn't take much to entice the bowlers; they came in numbers. On event day, we filled both sides of the center.

The tournament was as much instructional as it was competitive. Each team had a more experienced bowler serving as coach. I remember walking around the senior league asking for volunteers; almost everyone was supportive.

One quality I love about Andrew is his big-dream mentality. He's got the talent to match, but what makes it special is how generously he extends that belief to others. Impressed by what he saw in me on the lanes, he told me to make him a promise, that I'd qualify for my pro card and compete as a regional pro bowler. I told him my time had passed, that at this point it'd have to be in the senior division. He wasn't moved. Then seniors it is, he said without missing a beat.

What it is to see through a child's eyes. When do we trade that in, I wondered, for an emblem on the front of an overpriced car, or for the curb appeal that comes with a coveted zip code we once thought defined success?

It reminded me that I can learn a lot from Andrew. And no, I wasn't about to pursue a professional bowling career in my late forties, but I'd be lying if I said he didn't have me thinking about it for a minute or two.

Jarrod's tournament was a huge success. It sparked a surge of new bowlers, and for a while, a junior league formed that carried momentum. Eventually, it faded, but that didn't matter. The *Jarrod Kuhn Jr. Memorial League* had been a price-less event, a measure of success I could feel deep down. I was grateful for everyone who supported it.

Whether I was lost in thought or Dillon had naturally found a higher gear, some distance began to form between us. Maybe it was residual soreness from Freel, but I was decelerating, taking a moment to rest on a rock just off the trail. I rehydrated, tore into a Clif Bar, and refueled for the push I knew I'd need to catch up.

As I climbed higher, I spotted Dillon ahead, already exploring the rocky edges of Monument Peak. The summit wasn't a broad plateau like some others; it was a jagged crown of granite and sand. The final steps turned into a scramble, hands and boots working together until I pulled even with him near the top.

The view was magnificent, closer to the lake than Freel, yet still offering a sweeping curvature of Tahoe's shoreline, from Emerald Bay to Tahoe City. The alpine wilderness unfolded below us, ridgelines and valleys cascading in every direction. We took it all in, standing still for a while, until the thought of dinner back at camp broke the spell. The descent came faster, our pace now even, two hikers closing the loop on a Heavenly day.

WHERE PAIN BECOMES PRAYER

We'd been back from Tahoe a couple of months when the time had come to wrestle the finale of my second *Six Pack* of Peaks.

What *Backpacker Magazine* lists as one of the ten hardest day hikes in America is called Cactus to Clouds. It would be a return to San Jacinto, not starting from the drop point of the Aerial Tramway at 8,500 feet, but hiking that distance starting from the desert floor, up layer upon layer of cascading ridgelines.

Unlike Whitney, where the objective was clear, reach the top, C2C was more about making it to the Aerial Tramway landing. And if there was, by some miracle, enough time left in the day and strength in the legs, the hike would continue on to reach the clouds, the summit of San Jacinto, the second tallest point in Southern California. The rugged peak that had been my first "stone hammock" back during the first *Six Pack* of Peaks. From the summit, C2C routes you back down to the tram for a free ride to the desert floor.

Some, like the mystery man Erin and I saw at Grouse, proudly parading his second go in a row, actually return all the way to the museum on foot, extending C2C to C2C2C: *Cactus to Clouds to Cactus*. That's absurd, I thought. But then again, we all have our callings. Run with purpose in every step (1 Corinthians 9:26).

It was October, the ideal time to avoid the blistering temperatures this part of the desert is notorious for. The hike begins at the Palm Springs Art Museum, on the desert floor at an elevation of 480 feet. Our plan was to take the Skyline Trail, starting at midnight, so that we'd reach high enough to enjoy a sunrise to remember, and from there, stay above the scorching heat.

About that heat; this hike demands respect. Many have made the mistake of overheating or starting without the proper conditioning, deciding to turn back late morning, or worse, in the afternoon, only to meet the unrelenting furnace of air that hovers closer to the desert floor. That scenario often ends with a medevac, and tragically, it has overtaken some hikers over the years.

This would be a *Heaven Hike* for me, but I'd be joining a group, friends I knew and others I'd meet for the first time. C2C had already been an annual tradition for a few of them, which was reassuring. I'd be hiking in the dark with those who knew more than what was visible inside the small circle of light cast by their headlamps.

In my research, I'd read that the trail itself is difficult to follow in places. Still haunted by that lost moment near Freel, I was glad to follow rather than lead.

The numbers for C2C were both intimidating and inspiring. Our goal of reaching Long Valley would be an eleven-mile vertical grind, climbing nearly 8,000 feet. By comparison, Whitney starts at an elevation of about 8,300 feet, with just over 6,000 feet of gain to the summit. This one would be a hike to remember.

I wondered whether it would be a *Heaven Hike* in name only, walking as part of the largest group yet on my journey.

As I parked at the museum, a structure just a short walk from the start of the trail, I couldn't help but think back. It had been more than three years since my collision with a pair of hiking boots. As I was lacing them up, the same pair I'd worn on Mt. Wilson, the wear and tear told a story. Between the *Six Packs* and the hikes in between, I'd walked hundreds of miles and climbed tens of thousands of feet, grinding out the steps to reach the clouds.

A strange idea hit me in that moment. The pain and suffering on the trail seemed to be part of what opened the doorway to somewhere else, a place that felt closer to Jarrod. What I'd come to know as my very personal, heavenly visit.

I was reminded of Christ's suffering, the depth of pain He must have endured, unimaginable. He'd warned those closest to Him that knowing Him would also bring pain, but that to be close to Him meant closeness with the Father. *So then, those who suffer according to God's will should commit themselves to their faithful Creator and continue to do good.* (1 Peter 4:19)

There were times on the trail when a muscle in my mid-back would flare up, only when I pushed to reach farther. Once triggered, the pulsing pain would stay with me for the duration of the hike, lingering even afterward.

In some way, I thought, perhaps the deeper pain within me, the heartbreak and mental anguish, was transferring into my poles, down into the soles of my boots.

Was I being cleansed? Was the physical suffering the cost to purge my soul from the wasteland of grief it had become?

Those thoughts were already circulating even before the C2C hike began. One thing was certain; I'd be in for some of that mountain-variety pain and suffering on the trail today. Inexplicable as it was, I wasn't only prepared for it, I was looking forward to it. I was walking with a headlamp at midnight, ready to embrace every bit of what it had to offer in return.

We assembled quickly as a group. Ben, my best friend in the mix, greeted me with a smile and introduced me to the others. I hadn't met the organizer, John, until then, but I knew he'd set this whole thing up with an undeterred passion to reach the summit, to go all the way. There was a guy named Alex, a professional golfer I'd met briefly before but didn't know well.

Rounding out our group was someone I was seeing for the first time, shirtless under his pack, young and spry-looking. If we were taking bets at that point, mine would've been on him completing the challenge, with the rest of us happy enough to share a cold beer at the Aerial Tramway restaurant, living vicariously through his story when he got back.

It was serious business from the start. The trail didn't offer any relief on entry, right away it demanded negotiation through tight switchbacks carved into sharp rock, the path narrow and deliberate in its ascent. It was either John or Ben who set the pace for this stretch. With each upward turn, the distance between us and the glowing city lights below stretched farther away.

The Skyline Trail isn't maintained by the Forest Service, so what guides hikers are markers, spray-painted dots on boulders, left by determined trekkers over the years. We were generally following the white ones, indicating the main route. About two miles in, we reached our first milestone, a picnic bench and fitting spot for a brief respite.

By now, my legs had warmed up, not pain yet, more a settling comfort as my breathing caught up and the right muscles synced into that natural harmony with my poles. But the thought I'd had earlier stayed with me. It reminded me of a practice hike I'd done near home in Santa Ynez, a prep run before C2C.

The trail was called Gaviota Peak, a perfect blend of challenge and accessibility. Its summit revealed sweeping views of California's central coast, a reward that never failed to inspire. It had become one of my favorite hikes.

5/22/20

Revisiting a favorite - Heaven Hikes for Jr.

Jarrod Kahn

I remembered one particular day descending from the top. I might have been a little too brisk in my step, because that pinch in my back, normally kept at bay on this trail, flared suddenly.

I rounded a corner off the main switchbacks onto a wider dirt path that curved through golden mustard grass. The pain became unbearable, forcing me to stop and catch my breath. I shrugged off my pack and leaned on my poles for a minute, waiting for the pulsing to subside.

My eyes turned to the mustard, which I'd already admired on the way up for how lush and colorful it was; its distinct scent refreshing in the dry air.

Before me now was a beautiful monarch, and then another fluttered beside it. Either distracted just enough or captivated by their beauty, the pain in my back faded from persistence to memory. Then more butterflies came, different sizes, some smaller. They hadn't landed on the mustard, content to fly together in what looked like a playful dance, loosely orbiting one another as they drifted through the air.

I watched for a while, my thoughts turning to Jarrod, to those hugs he loved to give. And then, as quickly as they appeared, they were gone. A brief moment, but a healing one.

A gentle touch, heartfelt, offering relief from the pain in my back, however short that turned out to be.

As I kept on, the pain returned, but the warmth of that moment stayed with me. I walked with a smile and a spring in my step, calling out to my trail buddy who'd persevered at Freel, where he'd once written, "Ankle be damned."

On the drive back that afternoon, I was reminded of another time, similar, but on the bike. I'd extended my regular ride around the neighborhood, which always included a stretch alongside Jarrod's former elementary school.

Pushing it hard that day, with heat more brutal than usual, I was laboring by the time I reached the school. I decided to come off the bike, lean it against a tree, and take in some shade. Draining the last bit of water I had, I told myself home wasn't far.

As I was regaining my breath, a swirl of fallen leaves began to move in a way that caught my attention. It was a feeling hard to explain, but it brought a closeness with Jarrod that was unmistakable. Just at that moment, I glanced over at the tetherball court, his go-to spot on arrival before the first bell. The leaves soon scattered, and I was back on my bike, feeling calmer.

There were more of these encounters that felt real to me, moments I'd hesitate to share with others who might question my sanity. But they were private anyway, and told now only because they've become such a large part of the reward of *Heaven Hikes*.

We were a couple of hours in now when we reached Rescue Box 1, an enclosed metal box fixed to a wooden post, stocked by other hikers for anyone in need. We were about 3,500 feet above Palm Springs; the yellow and white lights dotted the valley below, flickering faintly in the distance.

We kept moving, probably looking like a cluster of fireflies drifting through the dark of night, all heading in one direction—up.

It wouldn't be long now before one of my favorite parts of any *Heaven Hike*, those fleeting minutes before dawn. The sunrise.

Just short of five miles from our start, now around 5,000 feet, the sun began to glow beyond the ridgeline. We stopped the longest here, each of us intent on taking in the same reward. No words, just deliberate movement as everyone found their own vantage point.

I was drawn to the way the light broke against the silhouettes of old pines, long passed but still standing, bleached white from years of sun and wind.

Their outstretched branches caught the light as if God had placed a spotlight on them, a muted song sung in wood and shadow. I thought of Kaitlyn, her beautiful voice, and our walk up "the mountain with a cross." *Music on the mountain*, I whispered to myself. *She would have loved this sight.*

Refreshed in mind and body, our group was ready to press onward, trading our firefly persona for a determined bunch of hikers pacing much slower than the gondola that would soon open above us.

Daybreak was revealing what lay ahead. The reality that the final third of this hike would be the true test came into view from our vantage point near Coffman's Crag. Another mile ahead and another thousand feet up and over. Visible now were the stacked, rolling ridgelines on the horizon, each one waiting its turn to be climbed.

We kept our pace, determined, each in our own thoughts, taking turns leading. Though much cooler than the basin below, or the trail already behind us, we were still exposed to the sun, and its heat was beginning to settle in.

What followed was a meditative sequence of climb, crest, descend slightly, then climb again, moving across layer upon layer of the mountain's ribs, like slow breaths rising and falling toward the sky.

Finally, we made our way over all of it, finding a place to rest with views of the coming transition, from the rough terrain of gravel and sand to what looked like an oasis of pines and firs. It was the wooded gateway into the alpine zone that would surround us the rest of the way.

A couple of miles back, Alex had begun showing signs of an empty tank, the distance between him and our small peloton stretching farther with every switchback. We'd never leave him behind; there was an unspoken grace in giving someone the space they needed to recover. We had plenty of time and no illusions at this point of summiting San Jacinto.

When Alex caught up, he was more vocal about his struggle, even talking about turning back. Although we all listened, that wasn't going to happen. We'd carry him before letting him descend. It was too dangerous. That's the cardinal mistake others have made.

It was humbling, for sure, but Alex was unassuming and genuinely pleasant to be around. He was more concerned about slowing us down, he said. A professional golfer who'd spent years in Colorado, he was no stranger to being physically tested, or to the high country, but he'd simply underestimated this one.

I had an idea. By now I'd learned that without my poles, I'd gas out on longer, more strenuous hikes. They weren't just useful for balance across uneven ground, or for avoiding an ankle or knee mishap; they were a way to share the load, transferring weight between arms and legs, giving each a break when needed.

I offered one of my poles to Alex. Maybe it was placebo, or maybe the right encouragement at the right time, but I'd convinced him it would help. Back in the form we started, into the trees we went.

We had long come of age, but as we trekked on, it felt more like a scene out of *Stand by Me*, Gordie, Chris, Teddy, and Vern walking through shaded woodlands, single file over fallen logs, the chatter of birds overhead and branches breaking under our feet.

Fewer words now, a steady pace of shared effort, hops, skips, and small bursts of joy from muscles that first came alive long ago.

Alex wasn't part of this wild, unspoken dance, but when I'd look back, he'd smile, give a leg kick, and raise his pole high, spirit unbreakable. Alex and I would become the kind of friends whose paths only cross now and then, but this hike always comes up. Bonding over the trail, grown-ups, but kids at heart, for a day.

Almost by surprise, new sights and sounds began to emerge ahead. As they grew clearer, one by one we pulled ourselves up the final stretch, over the ridge and onto the plateau. The observation deck of the tramway came into view. Families were scattered across it, kids playing, parents snapping pictures, everyone taking in the sweeping view of the Palm Springs skyline from more than 8,000 feet.

One family noticed us as we climbed up from below and looked startled. I could see it in their eyes... *Where did they just come from?* and maybe... *Why?*

We weren't there to answer either question. But for whatever reason, the hardest part of the entire day's hike was the final paved ramp leading up to the tramway restaurant. I'd almost forgotten about our shirtless hiker who had passed us hours earlier, aiming for the summit. I'm sure each of us came to San Jacinto for different reasons that day. It looked to me like the mountain gave what it could.

As I completed this second *Six Pack* of Peaks, *Heaven Hikes* had become more than unlocking memories of Jarrod, more than simply trying to relive a moment or hold on to each and every one. Those precious recollections still came often, but now they were part of something larger, a mosaic.

Memories from the past, imagined closeness in the present, visions of the future, all merging with thoughts of the new people in my life and the healing presence they carried with them.

Like the horizon of those ridgelines stacked one after another, I was intent to keep cresting, over one, then the next. Even knowing it was a summit I'd never fully reach, the journey itself would always be enough.

I was convinced that heavenly peak would come one day. I wasn't racing toward it, just loving the thought of it. For fun, I pictured a shirtless Jarrod waiting for me there, just like the old days when he'd torment his sister, grinning wide, ready with one of those signature hugs.

10
WHAT STAYS

There are far, far better things ahead than any we leave behind.

—C. S. Lewis
(The Collected Letters)

Even the darkest night will end and the sun will rise.

—Victor Hugo
(Les Misérables)

Therefore, if anyone is in Christ, the new creation has come: The old is gone, the new is here!

—2 Corinthians 5:17

It was actually Erin's idea for me to get a dog. A trail companion, she said. She had done her research and found that Australian Shepherds fit the job description well. They were working dogs, agile, smart, and friendly.

When Archie came home, he was an instant sensation. In those first couple of years as a puppy, we'd walk him on State Street in Santa Barbara. If we had plans to be someplace at a certain time, it wasn't happening. "Meatball," as we liked to call him, would stop traffic.

Later, when Archie was ready, I started taking him on moderate local hikes. He loved it, and I did too. I wasn't used to all the attention. His celebrity-like status followed him everywhere, even on the trail. Maybe he should run for mayor of Idyllwild, I thought. Give ol' Max a good challenge.

Archie has become much more than an occasional trail companion; he's a true friend. I believe dogs are a gift,

God's way of showing us what humility and unconditional love look like, pure and simple.

Mark Twain said it best when he described divine acceptance: "Heaven goes by favor. If it went by merit, you would stay out and your dog would go in."

POINTS OF INSPIRATION

Archie and I hiked Inspiration Point together often, a local out-and-back trail about four miles long, with roughly 1,000 feet of vertical gain. It's just enough effort to stay well-conditioned and to ease into that welcome, meditative state of mind. The hike is also, in no uncertain terms, Archie's limit, a fact he's made abundantly clear.

Inspiration Point is one of my regular *Heaven Hikes*. It offers an incredible lookout, and just beyond it, a less-traveled plateau with an even better vantage point. More rugged and usually unnoticed by hikers, it's the perfect refuge for reflection. This is my sweet spot.

On one of these hikes, my mind drifted to a book I'd just read, *Running with Raven*. It follows a man in Miami, known as Raven, who ran the same route every single day, without fail, for over forty years. Storms, illness, injury, and age never deterred his commitment.

Driven by a quest for meaning, purpose, and community, he simply kept moving. Over time, others, complete strangers, began joining him. Eventually, Raven became a source of inspiration to many.

I wondered if I could do something like that with my near-daily Inspiration Point hikes. I kept the thought to myself; Archie would have bailed at the mere suggestion. But after completing my second *Six Pack* of Peaks, I suppose I was already looking for my next challenge. It was a fun idea, I thought.

Mostly without Archie, I began my self-imposed streak. I hadn't picked a nickname; I figured that was for others to decide, and I told no one about the plan. Because of my travel schedule, I allowed for some flexibility, but I set my own "rules of engagement" to keep each hike comparable in effort and intention.

I actually made it forty-two days in a row at Inspiration Point itself, plus another eight days elsewhere, fifty days in total. Not forty years, but enough.

I eventually gave myself a nickname anyway, "Jay," as a nod to Jarrod's nickname, "J-Man," and to the Steller's Jay I'd seen at the start of the Mt. Wilson trail. Hats off to the Raven.

That brief experiment, my own version of the streak, led me to reflect on what *Heaven Hikes* had become. Were they a blend of personal triumph and intimacy, a reach into my heart, and a reach outward for something more? Could peace and adventure coexist?

The answers came through prayer and reflection. I came to believe that Jarrod would want me to enjoy the journey, the closeness with our newfound playground, whether those steps were taken with a heavy heart or a lighter spirit.

Either way, Jarrod would be with me every step of the trail, no less the healing ground that it had become.

Just like our rhythm in life, we would shuffle our feet in a harmony all our own, losing ourselves in quiet moments together, conversation born first of laughter, coming from a new adventure as much as from one we cherished together long ago.

Heaven Hikes was evolving, and so was I. More than healing. Not only surviving. I was living.

CONQUERED

With some inspiration from the Raven, I returned to Whitney. This time, the plan was an even earlier start. I'd take a page from the C2C playbook and arrive at the trailhead at midnight. That would give me plenty of time to reach the summit before any stormy conditions rolled in, or so I thought.

It turned out to be another humbling experience. I fell short again, forced to turn back halfway up the *99 switch-backs* as thunder and snow arrived earlier than expected.

I know people who've had clear skies on Whitney, who describe their climbs as difficult, yes, but pleasant enough, with no real danger. Not me. For me, this mountain had slipped through my fingers twice now.

Still, what I received that day made the hike worth every step. Leaving earlier positioned me higher than Mirror Lake for the sunrise.

I was mesmerized as the sun rose into view, framed perfectly between walls of stone, its light glowing against the rugged cliffs, creating a canopy of gold before my eyes. It felt as if the mountain itself had built a stage, the curtain had lifted, and the sun was performing for a private audience.

I felt Jarrod close beside me, as though we were watching together.

Perhaps that was the lesson that day. My journey toward heavenly closeness, my search to connect with Jarrod, began with those dark, often cold and uncertain mornings. But it was in embracing the sunrise that I learned what hope really looked like.

Sunrises became my source of truth, reminders that morning can be refreshing, that even after long nights, light always returns.

That truth was still forming in me, tested often by storms both within and without, but I was learning to wear the armor of renewal.

Walking down from Whitney that day didn't feel like defeat; it felt like triumph. *The sunrise was the summit.*

Edmund Hillary said it best:

It is not the mountain we conquer, but ourselves.

11
Rising Horizons

Tell me, what is it you plan to do with your one wild and precious life?

—Mary Oliver
(The Summer Day)

But those who hope in the Lord will renew their strength. They will soar on wings like eagles; they will run and not grow weary; they will walk and not be faint.

—Isaiah 40:31

Live the questions now.

—Rainer Maria Rilke
(Letters to a Young Poet)

Fourteen years later, and more than a couple pairs of hiking boots, I'm often asked what it's all meant. The question usually follows a simpler one: *Why do you hike so much?*

By now, I think that second question has been answered in the preceding pages, as it aligns with my own unfolding story. The first, though, is harder to put into words.

I can honestly say that I was once headed someplace very far from being captivated by sunrises. The force that pulled me out of that abyss is something I can't fully explain. But its source, the place where that power lives, I know in my heart to be Heaven.

My faith has always been a private one, less church pew, more silent prayer. I rarely spoke about my relationship with Jesus or the ways the Holy Spirit stirred within me, even before losing Jarrod. There was some shame in that, guilt even. In the years that followed, I cried out to God wondering if my silence had somehow led to punishment, if I hadn't done enough, if I had sinned too much.

If I've learned anything from this journey, it's that faith has opened my heart wider than I thought possible, and what's entered that space is a closeness with my son I could never have imagined.

As C.S. Lewis wrote of his own faith:

I believe in Christianity as I believe that the sun has risen, not only because I see it, but because by it I see everything else.

Any spiritual breakthrough I've experienced, what I've come to call *Heaven Hikes*, began as serene moments on the trail, simple feelings of warmth and closeness. Over time, those moments carried farther, lasting beyond the hike itself.

In the beginning, I rushed to the trail, eager for that vivid memory or unexpected encounter that might bring comfort. But as the years went on, the hikes became more sustaining.

I am still drawn to memories of Jarrod as he was in life, many of the same ones returning again and again, their joy undiminished. *Heaven Hikes* began by bringing those memories into focus when I needed them most.

They were soul-feeding, and they became a source of the strength it took to push against headwinds that once felt insurmountable, needed to survive what was unmistakably the darkest and most difficult season I have ever lived.

Later, those same hikes seemed to cut a new trail, one that opened pathways to memories yet to be lived, imagined as they might have unfolded with Jarrod growing up alongside me. Visions shaped by my mind's eye, but in my heart, they feel real and carry meaning. It's difficult to even put into words.

Hikes were ending at new beginnings.

Søren Kierkegaard's words began to speak truth to me: *Life can only be understood backwards; but it must be lived forwards.*

My journey has slowly moved from solitude toward openness, making space for others to reenter my life. What began as a way to endure became a way to live again. The trail did not erase grief, nor did it replace what was lost, but it gave me space to carry both memory and meaning forward together. *Heaven Hikes* taught me that movement does not mean leaving the past behind; it means learning how to walk with it.

Now, it's more like returning to the mountain, or walking along the beach to catch a restorative sunrise, a place to refuel. To be nourished by God's creation, heart full.

The message on my shoulder is always the same: keep moving. I continue on, step by step, not because the path is clear, but because it is still calling. Forward is still full of discovery and surprises, but the groundwork for a special connection has been laid. The trail remains a place where remembrance and hope can coexist, and where love, though changed, continues to move with me.

Often, when I look at the Sego in the backyard, I realize how far this journey has taken me. It's the same plant, full-grown now, that was only a few inches tall when Jarrod ran through the sliding door after school, backpack bouncing, keychains clinking, arms wrapping around me. Just like that Sego has grown, I like to think I have too.

Robert Frost once said he could sum up everything he'd learned about life in three words: *It Goes On.* Although the world did stop, my self-winding watch kept ticking. I can agree with Frost, *life does go on,* but for me, I've learned that I still need to keep winding that watch. That means to keep moving, to stay on the path.

I've come to believe that while life does go on, *where* it goes depends on more than chance.

I've found inspiration in Roosevelt's story, how he stayed ahead of his grief and rekindled light in his life. That way of thinking has guided my own version of "life goes on."

Yet I've also learned it takes more than my own strength. Just when I thought I couldn't love again, God placed people in my life, and they made it more than just carrying on.

I've been blessed with a family that loves me, people who surround me when my mind starts to wander toward darker paths.

Despite all that has come from *Heaven Hikes*, my faith, and the love that surrounds me, grief still finds a way in. Sometimes it comes in moments of weakness; sometimes, it ambushes me without warning. Every day, it's about staying the course, leaning on Erin, praying for strength, or hitting the trail. Sometimes, it takes everything.

LET'S WALK TOGETHER

Sharing *Heaven Hikes*, my story and Jarrod's memory, has been healing in itself. It's with my deepest gratitude that you've taken the time to read it. My prayer is that a few of the bread crumbs may carry meaning for you as well.

I remember how hungry I was for truth when I first set foot on this trail. That appetite remains, with the questions still outnumbering the answers. I am reminded by the incomplete view our earthly world offers when held against the heavenly promise to come, as reflected in 1 Corinthians 13:12:

For now, we see only a reflection as in a mirror; then we shall see face to face. Now I know in part; then I shall know fully, even as I am fully known.

Maybe Raven's vision can play out for *Heaven Hikes* after all. I learned in just a few weeks that I couldn't do it by myself. But I was reminded how Raven had attracted others who joined him, like-minded, encouraged, seeking something bigger than themselves.

The thought came to me. How wonderful would it be if that same community spirit carried forward, with someone, somewhere, every day, taking part in a *Heaven Hike*.

It's in this spirit that I invite you to hit the trail, or help spread the word. Not as a contest or something to be documented, but as a shared gesture of purpose. If you feel inclined, share a picture on *Heaven Hike's* Facebook page.

Perhaps together we can inspire and uplift others, helping them find closeness, healing, and peace of heart through time spent in nature.

Erin often reminds me that not everyone can climb a mountain, or even wants to. She's right. *Heaven Hikes* can be as simple and easygoing as a walk in the park or along the sand. I couldn't agree more.

With that, I look forward to seeing the pictures, especially if there's a sunrise, and even more so if they come with a short caption about what moved you. Whether it's a selfie, a group shot, or nature's beauty itself, all are welcome.

My hope is that you find what you're looking for, and that a walk in nature becomes an enlightening place to start, even if it isn't the only place you search.

I hope to see you on the trail. If not in person, then in spirit, moving together, in all our loveliness and loneliness, in that perfect harmony where hearts and minds open to let something amazing enter both.

As we end our time together, my parting message is that the journey of *Heaven Hikes* ends not with an answer, but with an invitation: to walk forward more aware, more attentive, and never alone. Each next step, each sunrise, moving with hope and grace toward heavenly closeness.

May God bless you in His creation, and may your heart find moments of peace as you continue your own journey forward

A Wife's Note by Erin Kuhn

When I first met Jarrod, I was already aware of the loss of his son, and even with that knowledge quietly present between us, I remember thinking that he was the strongest person I had ever known. That awareness did not come from anything he tried to explain or from any story he told, but from the way he refused to give up, from the courage it took to keep choosing life, and from the hope he carried as he learned how to open his heart again. At the time, I did not yet understand all the ways that grief had reshaped his life, but I could sense that the strength I was witnessing was not accidental; it was being built slowly, through faith and an ongoing willingness to remain open in a world that had already taken so much.

What struck me most was not simply that he survived, though that alone would have been remarkable, but that he was trying, with quiet intention, to build a life worth living again, a life his son would be proud of, and a life that could still hold purpose even in the aftermath of unimaginable loss. I was, and continue to be, deeply aware that this kind of perseverance is rare, and I remain in awe of his strength and fortitude in the face of what no parent should ever have to endure.

From my own limited understanding of grief at the time we met, I imagined that loving someone through loss would follow a pattern I could recognize, one shaped by visible sadness and moments of vulnerability that invited closeness. I assumed grief would make itself known in predictable ways, through tears at night, stories intimately shared, and moments where comfort could be offered and received. I thought that by listening closely and holding space with enough tenderness, I could help ease the weight of what he carried, not realizing then that grief does not always invite understanding, nor does it unfold in ways that feel familiar.

We did have nights when the grief was raw and obvious, but I soon learned that grief does not arrive neatly or predictably, nor does it wait for an appropriate moment or ask permission before entering a room. It reveals itself not only in the more obvious places, like holidays and birthdays, but also in quieter, more unpredictable ways, through a memory that surfaces without warning, a passing thought, a familiar song, or a moment spent watching other children reach milestones that gently but unmistakably reopen pain. Grief lives in sleepless nights and restless days, in exhaustion that lingers beneath the surface. It weaves itself into daily life in ways that are often invisible to others, but deeply and persistently felt by those who carry it.

I will not sugarcoat this journey, because there were times when the pain felt bigger than either of us or heavier than anything I knew how to hold. And yet, I promise you this: the journey is worth taking. To live a life alongside someone who possesses a profound appreciation for it, and a depth that can only come from having traveled through the roughest terrain, is something rare and deeply beautiful. Alongside the grief, I have watched a remarkable transformation of spirit unfold, one that has shaped a life now rooted in helping others. I have seen Jarrod ask the hardest and most honest questions a person can face, questions about why he is still here and what God has in store for the remaining years of his life. From those questions grew a steady resolve to use his story not as a source of despair, but as a bridge toward hope.

Before *Heaven Hikes* was something Jarrod could share or name, hiking was simply a means of survival. In the earliest days, it was not about purpose or helping others, but about staying alive, about putting one foot in front of the other when that was all he could do. He hiked alone, quietly and without explanation.

On the surface, it looked like exercise, something good for the mind and body, but beneath that simplicity was something far more urgent. He was climbing as high as he could, believing that each step upward brought him closer to his son in Heaven. He was breathing in what felt like spiritual air, finding just enough strength to leave the house, to keep moving, and to survive another day. Those early hikes were about choosing life in moments when hope felt fragile and about finding a place where grief could exist without consuming everything else.

As Jarrod continued on this deeply personal mission to climb toward his son in Heaven, he began to recognize the quiet and steady way nature was sustaining him along the way. During those solitary hikes, he found that being surrounded by nature allowed him to exist with his grief without needing to explain it or resolve it. The landscape itself seemed to speak to him in ways that words never could. The trees, shaped by years of weather and survival, reflected a strength that felt familiar, while the beauty of the plants and open spaces offered moments of calm when his thoughts felt heavy. Over time, Jarrod came to understand that he did not need to reach the highest mountain peak to be closer to Heaven, because God, in His mercy, had placed remnants of Heaven here on earth, woven into creation itself. In learning to connect to nature, he discovered a life-sustaining closeness to both God and Jarrod Jr. that has comforted him in ways nothing else could.

The true beginning of sharing *Heaven Hikes* was the family trip we took to The Narrows, because it marked the first time Jarrod felt able to share something that had sustained him so personally. That hike was not planned as the start of anything larger, but as a way to honor his son and to bring our family together in remembrance. Before we went, Jarrod asked that we dedicate the hike to Jarrod Jr., that we walk intentionally in his honor, and that we wear matching shirts as a symbol of unity and love. It was the first hike formally devoted to his memory, and it became a meaningful way to connect all of our children to him through shared experience. Walking together through God's creation, it felt as though his presence was there with us, woven quietly into the experience, allowing each of the children to feel close to him in their own way.

It was in the reflection of the Narrows hike that Jarrod began to speak gently and thoughtfully about what *Heaven Hikes* might one day become. He began to wonder what it could look like to invite others into this same kind of space, not to fix grief or ask people to explain their pain with words, but simply to walk together in honor of the people they love and miss. He talked about bringing family members, friends, churches, or small groups together, and even creating space for those who might need to walk alone, to hike with intention. From those conversations emerged the idea of *Heaven Hikes*, reflecting Jarrod's hope to create a space rooted in remembrance and faith, where even a single shared walk might bring comfort.

It is my hope that as you close this book, you feel less alone in your own grief, whatever form it may take, and that you feel gently invited into the healing power of nature and the faithful presence of God. I hope you find permission to grieve in your own way and on your own timeline, without comparison or expectation, and to trust that healing does not require forgetting, but remembering with love. If this journey has resonated with you, I invite you to stay connected with us through our *Heaven Hikes* Facebook group, where we share reflections, encouragement, and updates. Please feel free to reach out, to walk alongside us in whatever way feels right to you, and to stay tuned as this community continues to unfold. And most of all, I hope you carry this truth with you: even after devastating loss, love still remains, and the journey, though forever changed, can still hold meaning.

Erin Kuhn

An Invisible Risk

An Invisible Risk

It's always been difficult to talk about how Jarrod died and what led to him being at risk. This has stemmed from feelings of guilt for not asking the right questions or doing enough as his father and protector.

Jarrod was born without a spleen, a rarity that was unknown to us. When occurring at birth rather than the spleen's removal, the condition in Jarrod's case is referred to as congenital asplenia. An invisible risk.

Because congenital asplenia only exists in roughly one in hundreds of thousands or millions of births, it is not routinely screened for in newborns or with checkups unless a medical complication or family history draws attention to the spleen as a concern. It is merely considered statistically impractical to screen every newborn for it.

The condition is also usually absent any symptoms that would alert its existence. There is also generally nothing that presents in bloodwork that would identify the spleen is missing. A newborn can appear completely healthy, and the absence of a spleen unnoticed for years.

A simple abdominal ultrasound is normally enough to determine whether there is a spleen or not.

The spleen carries importance at any age, but it is especially vital in the first several years as the immune system matures. Early on, the spleen acts as a first line of defense, filtering bacteria from the bloodstream and producing antibodies. Without a spleen as a young child, the body is extremely vulnerable to catastrophic results from bacterial infections.

Jarrod was a healthy boy, who wasn't sick very often, nothing more than the occasional cold or flu, which he'd always recovered from in a matter of a few days at most. All appearances were that it was just another ordinary case of the flu one day when Jarrod came home sick from school.

Nothing serious, merely a low-grade fever, the usual body aches and fatigue that would suggest he'd caught the bug that was going around.

A few days after, Jarrod was up and about, looking and acting like his energetic self. All indications were that he was on the mend, having tackled it in due course, just as he always had before.

It would only be another 24 hours for Jarrod to regress from what turned out to be a bacterial infection to quickly develop into spinal meningitis. As the bacteria multiplied throughout Jarrod's bloodstream his compromised immune system was no match.

It's with the heaviest heart that I remember Jarrod's final hours but hoping now what I've learned may help others. Even though asplenia is extremely rare, my hope is that the resources available at the end of this book shine a light that is helpful. It's not medical advice, which I am not qualified to give, but references to information that I wish I knew when Jarrod was born.

Share your *Heaven Hikes* with us on
Facebook!

@HeavenHikes
(join community group)

Follow @HeavenHikes on these other socials:

Visit us at
HeavenHikes.com

Spleen Awareness
(Links to 3rd Party Medical Resources)

NOTICE: The resources accessed through this QR code are provided for general informational purposes only and are not intended as medical advice. Neither the publisher, VireoLex LLC, the author, Jarrod Kuhn, nor Heaven Hikes, LLC, provides medical diagnosis or treatment. Readers are encouraged to consult qualified healthcare professionals regarding individual medical questions or concerns.

Bonus Material
"Nighttime: A Different Kind of Motion"

Scan here to access this material
(unpublished chapter of *Heaven Hikes*)

Acknowledgements

Most of the hikes that fill these pages were me on the trails alone, in solitude, searching. Getting there, and staying the course, though, was not solo. It's only for the love and compassion, generously and kindly given, that I had the strength and courage to surrender, seek Heaven, and keep stepping forward.

Whether it was a hug, act of generosity when needed the most, word of affirmation, inspiration, encouragement or recognition, it landed in my heart where it rests now as an enduring source that pushes me to go farther, become closer, walk on the path to healing and a peaceful heart.

For all that has been given to me, and the countless blessings from God, my gratitude is immeasurable. The spirit behind this book is a humble attempt to be a continuation of that loving support received. My prayer is that our love, together, will shine through to others, and with God's grace, continue to multiply.

About the Author

Jarrod Kuhn splits his time between Southern California's Coachella Valley and the Central Coast, taking in the gifts of desert stillness and ocean light, cloud-piercing mountains and shore-hugging cliffs, enjoying as much of it outdoors as possible with his family, including one adventurous Aussie.

Readers can find him sharing moments from the trail and beyond on Facebook at *Heaven Hikes*. Thoughtful notes or quiet questions are always welcome via private message.

He also writes on business leadership, through titles such as *Leadership in Motion* and *Simply Sigma*.